BOWEL CANCER

The Essential Guide

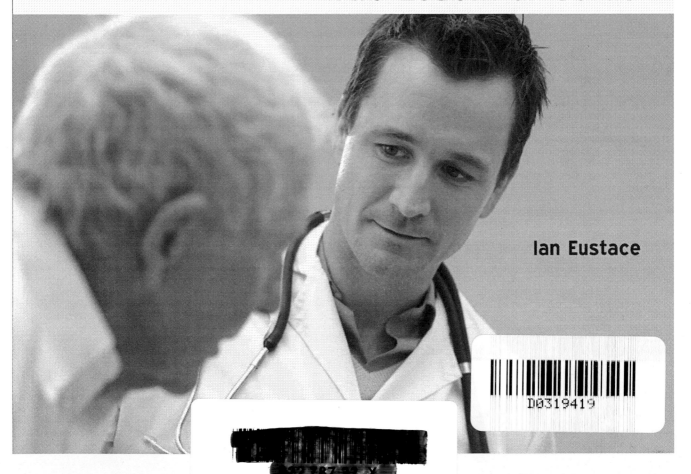

Ian Eustace

Bowel Cancer – The Essential Guide is also available in accessible formats for people with any degree of visual impairment. The large print edition and eBook (with accessibility features enabled) are available from Need2Know. Please let us know if there are any special features you require and we will do our best to accommodate your needs.

First published in Great Britain in 2011 by
Need2Know
Remus House
Coltsfoot Drive
Peterborough
PE2 9BF
Telephone 01733 898103
Fax 01733 313524
www.need2knowbooks.co.uk

Contents

Introduction

There are few words in the English language that can provoke such powerful emotions and reactions as the word 'cancer' does, however information is critical to allow us to understand what having cancer actually means for ourselves, our families and friends, and the future. Nowadays, we understand a lot more about cancer; doctors can diagnose the disease earlier, treatments are getting better all the time, and many cancers can be cured.

This book has been written to inform anyone interested in reading about bowel cancer. It is also intended to help those who are diagnosed with the disease, family and friends who want as much information as possible about the causes, symptoms and treatment of bowel cancer, and to describe what the outcome is likely to be.

Here are some facts about bowel cancer:

- Bowel cancer affects more than 37,000 people in the UK every year and is the third most common cancer.

- Bowel cancer does not appear to be on the increase, diagnosis is being made earlier through screening programmes, and treatments are getting better.

- Bowel cancer can be managed very effectively to allow people to lead as normal a life as possible for as long as possible.

- The symptoms of bowel cancer are shared with many other conditions that are far less serious, such as haemmorrhoids (piles). The majority of people who have symptoms similar to those of bowel cancer do not have cancer.

- Bowel cancer tends to develop in older people – about 80% of cases are diagnosed in people aged 60 or above.

It is important to remember that the symptoms of bowel cancer are shared with many other conditions that are far less serious. This book is aimed at reassuring those of us who are worried that they might have cancer but, in fact, screening programmes and clinical studies tell us that in most of the cases, cancer is not the cause of their symptoms.

For those who have been diagnosed with bowel cancer, this book contains practical information about your treatment choices and how to cope with cancer on a daily basis. For healthy individuals it also gives valuable information about what you can do to reduce the risk of developing bowel cancer and gives useful tips on healthy eating and lifestyle.

Disclaimer

This book has been written to give you general information only and is not intended to replace medical advice. You should see your GP for individual medical advice about treatment of bowel cancer or any worries or concerns you might have. The factual material for this book is taken from many sources, all of which are listed in the help list. All facts and figures are as up to date as possible, but for further information please refer to these sources.

Chapter One

What is Bowel Cancer?

The word 'cancer' can provoke a number of emotions and responses, but it is very important to have accurate information about this disease. Talking about your bowels or going to the toilet can be very embarrassing and it may be very hard to ask questions, however with the right information it should be easier to discuss this sensitive subject with your doctor.

In this chapter you will find all of the basic facts about bowel cancer so you will be well prepared for anything you might have to deal with, whether this is prevention or treatment. Further chapters in this book will provide you with more information.

The help list at the end of the book gives information on where to access help and support.

What is the bowel?

The bowel is part of the digestive system (see overleaf). The digestive system is often called the gastrointestinal (GI) tract and consists of the mouth, food pipe or gullet (oesophagus), stomach, small bowel (small intestine) and large bowel (colon and rectum). The GI tract extracts all of the nutrients and water from the food we eat that our bodies need. Food is passed from the mouth to the stomach, where it is digested and passed into the small bowel. Here, essential nutrients are extracted from the food. As the food passes into the large bowel, water is absorbed leaving just the waste (stool, faeces or poo), which is passed out of the body through the back passage (rectum) via the anus.

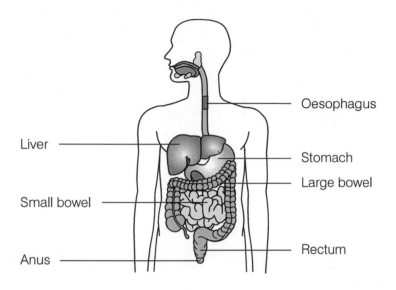

Oesophagus

Liver

Stomach

Large bowel

Small bowel

Rectum

Anus

The small bowel

The small bowel is the part of GI tract that is immediately beyond the stomach (See opposite). It is called the small bowel because it is narrower than the large bowel, but is the longest section of the GI tract (about 20 feet in total).

The large bowel

The large bowel is the last part of the GI tract and consists of the colon and rectum. The colon begins at the point where it is joined to the small bowel (where the appendix is located), runs up the right side of the trunk (abdomen). This part of the colon is called the ascending colon. It then crosses the body underneath the stomach (transverse colon) before travelling down the left side of the abdomen (descending colon), where an S-shaped bend (the sigmoid colon) leads to the rectum (which joins the anus, the external opening of the bowel). The colon therefore has five distinct sections and is about five feet long in total.

The small and large bowel are surrounded by a sheet of tissue known as the mesentery, which contains blood vessels that supply blood to the bowel and lymph nodes that drain away tissue fluid from the rectum.

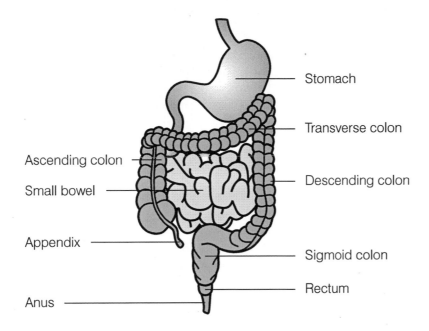

Stomach

Transverse colon

Ascending colon

Small bowel

Descending colon

Appendix

Sigmoid colon

Rectum

Anus

Cancer

Cancer is caused when the normal process of replacement of cells in the body becomes uncontrolled. The cells continue to divide and form a growth known as a tumour. However, a tumour is not necessarily cancer, which is considered to be a tumour whose cells spread to other parts of the body. These benign tumours can cause problems if their size causes them to press on surrounding tissues, for example in the brain.

A malignant or cancerous tumour contains cells that spread to other parts of the body, usually in the blood or the lymphatic system. Cancers are described by the location of the malignant tumour (the primary site), for example bowel cancer, lung cancer, breast cancer, skin cancer and many others.

Cells that spread from the primary tumour can form tumours in other parts of the body and these are known as secondary tumours or metastases. Further information about secondary tumours can be found later in this book.

What is bowel cancer?

The term 'bowel cancer' generally refers to cancer of the large bowel (colon and rectum). You may hear doctors use the term 'colorectal cancer' to describe it. Cancer does occur in the small bowel, although it is extremely rare. The cancer growth is usually called a tumour.

How does it develop?

The bowel consists of walls made of several layers of tissue. Bowel cancer starts on the inner wall and it is thought that it develops over 5-10 years. Most cancers start as a small growth called a polyp or adenoma on the inner bowel wall. If they are left undiagnosed and untreated they can spread to the other layers of the bowel and eventually to parts of the body outside the bowel such as the womb, prostate gland and bladder.

The lymphatic system consists of vessels and swellings called lymph nodes. The lymphatic system carries fluid to and from our body tissues and is also part of the body's immune system. Bowel cancer can spread through the lymph nodes as these are plentiful in the abdomen close to the bowel and this is one of the first places that bowel cancer can spread to.

In addition, bowel cancer cells can travel through the bloodstream to other more distant parts of the body and form cancers in other sites. This is called metastatic spread. The liver is a common site for metastatic cancer to develop as blood from the bowel goes directly to the liver.

Types of bowel cancer

There are five types of bowel cancer and they are classified according to the type of tissue that they develop in:

- Adenocarcinoma. This is the most common type of bowel cancer. Over 95% of cases are adenocarcinoma. These tumours begin in the gland cells (cells that produce mucus to help move the stool through the bowel) of the bowel lining. Adenocarcinomas can be described as either mucinous or signet ring depending upon how the cells appear under the microscope. Mucinous tumours contain cancer cells in pools of mucus. Signet ring tumours consist of cells that contain mucus which pushes the nucleus to one side of the cell, giving it a signet ring-like appearance.

- Squamous cell carcinoma. These originate in the cells that line the bowel. Unlike gland cells, squamous cells do not produce mucus and are similar to skin cells.

- Sarcomas. These are tumours of the supporting cells of the body, such as muscle and bone. Sarcomas that arise in the muscle of the bowel are known as leiomyosarcomas.

- Carcinoid tumours. These are rare types of neuroendocrine tumour, meaning that they develop in organs or tissues that produce hormones, usually in the GI tract. Between 4 and 17% of carcinoid tumours start in the rectum, 2-7% in the large bowel

- Lymphomas. These are tumours of the lymphatic system and are rare – only about 1% of bowel cancers are lymphomas.

How common is bowel cancer?

Bowel cancer is currently the third most common cancer in the UK. It is the second most common cancer in women after breast cancer and the third most common cancer in men after prostate and lung cancer. Every year over 37,000 people (about 20,400 men and 17,000 women) are diagnosed with bowel cancer. In 80% of cases people are aged 60 and over. However, the rate at which new cases occur (incidence) has remained stable over the last ten years, so bowel cancer does not appear to be on the increase. The incidence rates of bowel cancer vary throughout the world. The lowest incidence rates are seen in South Central Asia and Eastern, Western, Northern and Middle African countries. The highest rates are in Europe, North America and Australasia.

Causes of bowel cancer

We do not know precisely why cells should start to divide out of control and become cancer cells however research around the world has identified a number of risk factors for bowel cancer. While these risk factors are associated with the development of bowel cancer it is important to remember that they do not necessarily cause bowel cancer – they just increase the likelihood of getting bowel cancer. You should also remember that if you have cancer you may not necessarily have any or all of these risk factors.

Risk factors for bowel cancer

Some risk factors can be altered (modifiable) to change the level of risk whilst others cannot be altered (non-modifiable). Examples of modifiable risk factors include diet and lifestyle. You can alter your diet to make it healthier and you can improve your lifestyle by exercising and maintaining a healthy weight. Age and family history are examples of non-modifiable risk factors; in other words these are risk factors that you cannot change.

Age

The biggest risk factor for bowel cancer is age. More than 80% of bowel cancer cases are diagnosed in people over the age of 60.

Family history

A family history of bowel cancer also increases the risk, especially if a close relative (a parent, brother, sister or child) from the same side of your family is diagnosed with bowel cancer under the age of 45, or if two close relatives are diagnosed regardless of how old they are.

Inherited conditions

There are also some inherited conditions that can increase the risk of bowel cancer. Lynch syndrome or hereditary non-polyposis colorectal cancer (HNPCC) is a rare genetic condition which increases the risk of getting many types of cancer, including bowel cancer. The HNPCC gene is involved in the repair of DNA in our body cells. People with Lynch syndrome have a fault (or mutation) in the HNPCC gene which results in a lifetime risk of developing colon cancer of about 80%. Women with Lynch syndrome also have an 80% lifetime risk of developing endometrial cancer (cancer of the lining of the womb or uterus).

Familial adenomatous polyposis (FAP) is a disease that causes the growth of numerous polyps in the large bowel. Most are non-cancerous (benign) but some can develop into cancer with time. The risk of getting bowel cancer is higher in people with FAP because of the number of polyps, and most will develop bowel cancer by age 40-50. Because of this, people with FAP may have surgery to remove the entire colon (colonectomy) at age 25 to reduce the risk of bowel cancer. FAP is very rare with only one in 7,000 people (less than 1%) with bowel cancer having the condition.

Turcot syndrome is a condition similar to Lynch syndrome and FAP. It is a condition associated with faulty DNA repair that leads to gene mutations and the formation of polyps in the bowel. Turcot syndrome affects the same genes involved with Lynch syndrome and FAP. Turcot syndrome is rare; both Lynch syndrome and FAP are more common.

Chronic diseases of the bowel

Chronic (long-lasting) diseases of the bowel can also increase the risk of bowel cancer.

Ulcerative colitis is an inflammatory bowel disease (IBD), in other words it causes irritation, swelling and the formation of ulcers (open sores) in the lining of the colon. People with ulcerative colitis have bouts of diarrhoea which contains blood from the ulcers that may last for weeks. The cause is not known although there are links to genetics and a diet low in fibre. There is an increased risk of bowel cancer in people who have had ulcerative colitis for 10 years or more in the colon beyond the splenic flexure (the bend between the transverse and descending parts of the colon). Approximately 1% of bowel cancers develop as a result of ulcerative colitis.

Like ulcerative colitis, Crohn's disease is an inflammatory bowel disease, although it can affect the entire GI tract from the mouth to the anus. About half of the people with Crohn's disease have inflammation and ulcers in both the small and large bowel, whilst about 20% have Crohn's just in the large bowel. The disease causes chronic inflammation of the bowel and severe episodes cause repeated damage to the bowel lining. People with Crohn's disease have about a two and a half-fold increased risk of getting bowel cancer.

Ethnic risk factors

Ashkenazi Jewish people (those of Eastern European descent) have an increased risk of bowel cancer (two to three times higher than the general population). This partly explains why colorectal cancer is the most common cause of cancer deaths in Israel and is thought to be due to a mutation called I1307K of the APC (adenomatous polyposis coli) gene. The mutation is present in about 10% of Ashkenazi Jews and a mutated APC gene actually causes the cancer to grow rather than helping to prevent it.

Diabetes

People with diabetes are more likely to develop bowel cancer, but as yet we do not know why. People with type 2 diabetes (those who are not dependent upon insulin injections) share some of the same risk factors (including obesity) as those for bowel cancer, but even when these shared risks factors are taken into account, people with type 2 diabetes still have an increased risk and their outcome after diagnosis is likely to be poorer.

Diet

Certain foods have been linked to an increased risk of bowel cancer. Eating large amounts of red and processed meat appears to increase the risk of bowel cancer. This is thought to be due to the observation that there are certain chemicals present in red meat that might increase cancer risk. One such substance called haem gives the meat its red colour but is thought to cause damage to the lining of the colon. Processed meat is treated to preserve it using methods such as curing, smoking, salting, or adding chemicals, and it is thought that these processes can result in the formation of carcinogens (cancer-causing chemicals). The cooking of meat at high temperature (for example by roasting or frying) is also thought to result in the production of chemicals that can cause bowel cancer.

Certain types of fat, especially saturated fat (found in red meat and dairy products such as butter and cheese) and trans-fats (found in processed food) are thought to be linked to the formation of polyps.

People who have a diet that is low in fibre (plant-based food also known as roughage) have an increased risk of bowel cancer. Fibre increases intestinal transit (the speed at which food moves through the bowel) and ensures that your bowel movements are regular. Not having enough fibre in the diet slows down intestinal transit, meaning that potentially harmful chemicals are in contact with the cells lining the bowel for longer. Low fibre diets might also result in constipation, where the stools become hard and more difficult to pass. To highlight the importance of fibre in the diet, traditional native Japanese people have a diet that is naturally high in fibre and they have a lower risk of bowel cancer compared with people living in Western Europe. However, those Japanese people who have migrated to the West and have taken up a Western-style diet have the same risk of getting bowel cancer as Western people. In other words, by changing their diet from high fibre to low fibre, their risk of bowel cancer increases.

'There is still a risk of bowel cancer even with alcohol consumption that is below the recommended weekly limits for men and women.'

Smoking

If you smoke you have a higher risk of developing many types of cancer (especially lung cancer) including bowel cancer. Your risk is also higher if you are an ex-smoker compared with somebody who has never smoked.

Alcohol

Drinking large amounts of alcohol (in other words well above the weekly allowances of 21 units for men and 14 units for women) appears to increase the risk of colorectal cancer. Some very recent research published in April 2011 in the British Medical Journal showed that one in 10 cancers in men and one in 33 in women in Europe are caused by alcohol. The research also shows that there is still a risk of bowel cancer even with alcohol consumption that is below the recommended weekly limits for men and women and even those who were previously drinkers have a higher risk.

Lifestyle

'There are strong links between obesity, low physical activity and increased risk of bowel cancer.'

Low physical activity and obesity also appear to be associated with increased risk of developing bowel cancer. People who do not exercise appear to have poorer intestinal transit compared with people who exercise regularly. The longer that food remains in the gut, the higher the chance that the cells of the bowel will be exposed to potentially harmful chemicals.

A large study of more than 500,000 people in Europe is being conducted to determine the relationships between cancer and diet, lifestyle, nutritional status and the environment. This study is known as the European Prospective Investigation into Cancer and Nutrition (EPIC) study. The key findings of this study so far support observations of other studies showing that there are strong links between obesity, low physical activity and increased risk of bowel cancer.

Obesity is defined as a medical condition in which so much body fat has been gained that it threatens people's health and is usually measured by a tool called the Body Mass Index (BMI). This takes measurements of body weight and height and gives a number which represents the weight in terms of body surface area in square metres (kg/m^2). Healthy individuals have a BMI of less than 25; those that are overweight have a BMI of between 25 and 30, whilst obesity is associated with a BMI of more than 30. However, it is important to remember that BMI is only a guide and it does not take into account differences in build. You can be fit and healthy but still have a BMI that suggests you are overweight if you are heavily built. Most male rugby players would be overweight according to BMI because of their bigger build, even if they have very little body fat.

There is also a strong link between lack of exercise and weight gain, as those people who do not exercise do not use up enough energy to maintain a healthy weight. If you are overweight the likelihood is that you may be eating too much of the wrong types of food. For more information about weight and related subjects see *Weight Loss – The Essential Guide* (Need2Know).

A word about genetics

Genetics is the study of inherited characteristics. Every cell in our body contains a blueprint of our genetic material and all of this information is contained within a molecule known as DNA (deoxyribonucleic acid). The cells in our body are constantly dividing, for example our skin cells and the cells lining the bowel are continually replacing dead cells or cells that are lost from the body. Every time these cells divide the DNA they contain is copied resulting in two identical cells with the same genetic material. DNA is composed of smaller molecules called bases and strings of these different bases are called genes and are responsible for the production of different types of proteins and other substances that our cells need to function normally.

Genetics is important in many cancers, including bowel cancer, for a number of reasons:

- The cells in the lining of the bowel are rapidly dividing; the rate at which they divide is faster than that of many other types of cell in the body

- Every time a cell divides the DNA inside it is copied. Mistakes in this copying process (mutations) do happen and this can result in a faulty gene that produces a faulty protein or other substance which does not behave as it should.

- Some of the genes in our DNA have been linked to bowel cancer (these are sometimes called oncogenes or tumour promoter genes) and these can be overactive or mutated in people who have the disease. The APC protein is an example of an oncogene as a mutation of this gene called I1307K increases the risk of bowel cancer in Ashkenazi Jewish people. Oncogenes are involved in some way with cell division or replication.

- Because mistakes are made during the copying of DNA when cells divide, there are natural processes that are designed to recognise these mistakes and correct them. Some genes are responsible for making DNA repair proteins which can repair the damage caused by mistakes in DNA copying, or they can stop mutated cells from dividing and replicating (these are sometimes called tumour suppressor genes).

- Cells that are abnormal are also controlled by a 'self-destruct' mechanism known as apoptosis, or programmed cell death, where they effectively commit suicide. Apoptosis is controlled by a complex system of genes and proteins.

Normally, the rate at which mutations happen during the DNA copying process is controlled by the genes that produce repair proteins. In this way there are natural controls that ensure that all cells our bodies produce are normal and function properly. By their nature, cancer cells are those that divide in an uncontrolled manner, meaning that the natural control mechanisms are not working properly. One way of looking at this is imagining a see-saw, with tumour suppressor genes on one side and oncogenes on the other side. Normally, each process balances the other and the see-saw is level (A). However, if either the repair process is damaged in some way so that it does not work properly (this might be caused by a mutation in the gene for the DNA repair proteins) or the number of faulty proteins produced through mutation increases (oncogenes become overactive – B), this can affect the normal control of rapidly dividing cells and can mean that the possibility of the cells becoming cancerous is increased (See below).

> 'Outcomes for people with bowel cancer are improving all the time and the outlook is especially good for people who are diagnosed early.'

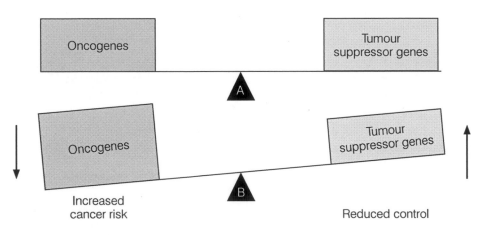

In reality, the science of genetics is much more complicated than the simple concept outlined here, but what it shows is the importance of genetics in the development of conditions such as bowel cancer, and hopefully should give you some insight into understanding the importance of genetics and cancer. Researchers are now using their knowledge of the genetics of bowel cancer to increase their level of understanding on how the cancer develops and to create better treatments that are able to target cancer cells and not healthy cells.

What is the outcome likely to be for people with bowel cancer?

Outcomes for cancers are usually expressed in terms of survival rates over time (commonly five years) from diagnosis. The five year survival rate depends on a number of different factors, such as age, and how early the diagnosis is made. Overall, approximately 50% of people diagnosed with bowel cancer will survive at least five years from diagnosis. Five year survival rates for patients diagnosed at the earliest stage are thought to be over 90%, whilst younger patients have a better outcome (prognosis) than older people.

In 2007 there were approximately 16,000 deaths from bowel cancer in the UK. However, the death rate has been falling continuously since the early 1990s; between 1998 and 2007, bowel cancer mortality rates have decreased by 16%. With better treatment and earlier diagnosis, the mortality rates are likely to continue to fall.

Summing Up

- The word 'cancer' is frightening and can provoke intense emotions and reactions. However, our knowledge of cancer nowadays is far better than it used to be and treatments are more effective. As a result the outlook for people with cancer is better.

- When we talk about bowel cancer, this usually means the large bowel (colon and rectum).

- You can help yourself, your family or friends by being well informed about bowel cancer.

- We do not know exactly why many people get bowel cancer, but there are some risk factors that have been identified that can increase the risk of getting the disease. There also seems to be a genetic link to bowel cancer.

- Outcomes for people with bowel cancer are improving all the time and the outlook is especially good for people who are diagnosed early.

Chapter Two

Prevention of Bowel Cancer

They say that prevention is better than cure and there are a number of ways to minimise the risk of getting bowel cancer and to reduce the potential impact of some of the risk factors that are mentioned in chapter 1.

Bowel cancer screening

Screening refers to looking for early signs of a disease in otherwise healthy people who do not have any symptoms. In the UK there are a number of different screening programmes in place for bowel cancer. In England the National Health Service (NHS) runs a bowel cancer screening programme (BCSP) that began in 2006 and has now achieved nationwide coverage. Since the risk of bowel cancer increases with age, all people aged 60-69 are sent a stool testing kit to test for blood (faecal occult blood or FOB test) every two years. People over the age of 70 can contact the NHS BCSP to request the screening kit. People in Wales are given FOB tests every two years from age 60-69 and in Scotland every two years from age 50-74. A screening programme was started in Northern Ireland in April 2010 and is offering tests every two years to people aged 60-69.

The FOB test is simple to use. You will need to collect small samples of your stools and wipe them onto a test card, which is then sealed and sent to a laboratory for analysis. You will normally be informed of the results within a fortnight. Full information on how to use the test kit is provided on the NHS bowel cancer screening programme website (see help list).

'Screening refers to looking for early signs of a disease in otherwise healthy people who do not have any symptoms.'

The proportion of abnormal results (positive FOB tests) is small (only about 2%) and the presence of blood in the stools does not necessarily imply that the cause is cancer. By contrast a negative test does not rule out bowel cancer, so be aware of the symptoms of bowel cancer and see your GP if you are at all worried. People with an abnormal result will be invited to attend a bowel screening centre, where a more detailed examination will be carried out and colonoscopy may be offered. In this procedure a small flexible tube with a light and camera (endoscope) is passed into the rectum and up into the colon to check for any abnormalities (See below).

The procedure is used to examine the full length of the colon and the doctor can look at the lining of the colon on a monitor as the endoscope passes along. Colonoscopy is carried out at a hospital as a day case (meaning that you can go home on the same day after having the test). You will be asked to stick to a special diet, be given laxatives and asked to drink plenty of water in the days before the test as the bowel needs to be completely clear of faeces. Just before you have the colonoscopy you will be given a sedative (a drug designed to relax you) and the procedure normally lasts between 30 minutes and an hour.

About 20 people in every 1,000 will be asked to do the FOB test for a second time. Sixteen of those are likely to be given a colonoscopy, of which about eight will have no abnormalities, about six will have polyps and about two will have cancer.

Bowel cancer usually develops slowly from polyps and a clinical trial in the UK using flexible sigmoidoscopy (an endoscope used to examine only the lower part of the large bowel, the sigmoid colon) and removal of any polyps found with surgery showed that this type of screening could prevent bowel cancer from developing. The study was very large and included more than 170,000 patients, just over 40,000 of which were given a single flexible sigmoidoscopy and were followed for 11 years. The results of this clinical trial showed that, in those people who had the sigmoidoscopy screen, the incidence of colorectal cancer was reduced by 33% and mortality (deaths) by 43%. The study concluded that flexible sigmoidoscopy screening offered once to people aged between 55 and 64 years is highly beneficial and offers long-lasting protection from colorectal cancer.

Flexible sigmoidoscopy is a similar procedure to the colonoscopy outlined above, but it is quicker (usually no more than about 25 minutes) as only the lower part of the large bowel (sigmoid colon and rectum) are examined. Preparation for flexible sigmoidoscopy is similar to colonoscopy. You will be given an enema before the

'Flexible sigmoidoscopy screening offered once to people aged between 55 and 64 years is highly beneficial and offers long lasting protection from colorectal cancer.'

procedure to flush any faeces from the sigmoid colon and rectum. In some cases you may be asked to follow a special diet in the days leading up to the test if the GI tract needs to be completely clear.

Modifying risk factors

In chapter 1 the concept of modifiable and non-modifiable risk factors was introduced. This section examines the risk factors for bowel cancer that can be modified to reduce the risk of getting the disease.

Diet

Guideline daily amounts

The Food and Drink Federation has produced a series of Guideline Daily Amounts (GDAs) to help to give guidance on how many calories and nutrients people should consume per day for a healthy, balanced diet. The table below summarises the GDAs for calories, protein, carbohydrate, sugars, fat, saturates (saturated fat), fibre and salt.

Guideline Daily Amount Values			
Typical values	Women	Men	Children (5-10 years)
Calories	2,000 kcal	2,500 kcal	1,800 kcal
Protein	45g	55g	24g
Carbohydrate	230g	300g	220g
Sugars	90g	120g	85g
Fat	70g	95g	70g
Saturates	20g	30g	20g
Fibre	24g	24g	15g
Salt	6g	6g	4g

Guideline daily amounts for men, women and children. Reproduced with kind permission of the FDF.

The GDA values are based on those for a physically active person of healthy weight, but they are guides, not targets. Some people may need to eat more or less than the GDA amount according to their gender, weight, activity levels and age, although it is recommended not to exceed the GDA for calories, sugars, fat, saturates and salt.

Many foods are now labelled with information on nutritional value and the proportion of the GDA amount that the food contains. This information helps you to make informed decisions about choosing foods for a healthier, more balanced diet.

Meat

'A diet that contains fibre is essential to keep your bowels healthy and functioning properly.'

Red meat, especially processed red meat, has been shown to increase the risk of bowel cancer. This does not mean that you should stop eating red meat completely, but consuming red meat in moderation is sensible. The Department of Health recommends that if you currently eat more than 90g of red meat in one day you should try to cut this down to the UK average of 70g a day. To put this into perspective, 70g is about equal to two standard beef burgers or three slices of ham.

As an alternative to red meat, try to include more white meat such as chicken and turkey, and more fish in your diet. These are high in protein and contain less fat than red meat. One of the key findings of the EPIC study is that eating fish probably reduces the risk of developing bowel cancer, though this has not been proven for definite.

Fibre

A diet that contains fibre is essential to keep your bowels healthy and functioning properly. Fibre (also previously known as roughage) comes from plant-based foods and cannot be digested by the human body. The main function of fibre is to speed up the removal of waste and toxins, preventing them from staying in the bowel for too long, which can increase the likelihood of bowel cancer. Fibre can be either soluble or insoluble.

Soluble fibre absorbs water in the bowel and helps to make the stools softer and easier to pass. It also reduces cholesterol and helps to control blood sugar levels. Soluble fibre is found in fruit and vegetables with apples, strawberries and legumes being rich sources.

Insoluble fibre consists mainly of a substance called cellulose, which the human body is completely unable to digest. Insoluble fibre makes the stools soft and bulky and quicker and easier to pass out of the body, preventing constipation.

Sources of soluble and insoluble fibre are summarised in the table below. You will see that some foods such as beans and oats contain both soluble and insoluble fibre.

Soluble fibre	Legumes (peas, beans, lentils, peanuts) Apples Citrus fruit (oranges, lemons, limes) Pears Strawberries Oats Barley Potatoes Soya products
Insoluble Fibre	Beans Lentils Oats Maize Bran Brown rice Wholegrain bread and cereals Wholemeal bread, cereals and pasta Wholemeal flour Seeds Nuts

Sources of soluble and insoluble fibre

The recommended guideline daily amount for fibre intake for adults per day is 18g, although according to the British Nutrition Foundation the average daily fibre intake in the UK is 12g, meaning that most of us do not have enough fibre in our current diets.

How much fibre does food contain?

If you need to increase the amount of fibre in your diet, then it is useful to have an idea of how much fibre commonly eaten foods contain. The next table shows a summary of popular foods and the average amount of fibre that they contain. Some foods are labelled as 'high fibre' but these must contain at least 6g of fibre per 100g weight or 100ml volume. Similarly, there are foods that are labelled 'source of fibre' and these must contain at least 3g of fibre per 100g weight or 100ml volume.

Food type	Portion size	Fibre content (g)
Cereal (e.g. Bran Flakes, Fruit & Fibre)	One bowl (30g)	4-7
Wholemeal bread	One slice	3-4
White bread	One slice	0.8
Pasta (wholewheat)	One portion (90g)	9
Lentils	One portion (80g)	1.5
Fruit: Apple Orange Banana Figs (dried)	Whole fruit Whole fruit Whole fruit 50 g	2g 2-3 4g 3.8
Peanut butter	Tablespoon	1.5
Baked beans	Small tin (200 g)	7.7
Baked potato (with skin)	Whole potato	5
Cabbage (boiled)	80 g	1.7

Approximate fibre content of a range of foods

Fibre is an essential part of a good balanced diet, but just like other foods, too much fibre can be bad for you, causing you to become deficient in minerals such as iron, calcium and zinc. If you want to increase the amount of fibre in your diet it is better to build up slowly to avoid these problems. An increase of no more than 5g in a week is probably a good idea. Notice the difference in fibre content between white and wholemeal bread. Wholemeal bread contains between four and five times as much fibre per slice as ordinary white bread, so simply switching from white to wholemeal bread can make a big impact on your daily fibre intake.

The key findings of the EPIC study have shown that a high fibre diet reduces the risk of bowel cancer. Fibre seems to help prevent the growth of polyps and also their transformation into cancer. In addition, it seems that there are also additional gains from a high fibre diet. A very recently published study (April 2011) conducted by the National Institute of Health in the USA showed that people who had between 25 and 30g of fibre in their daily diet were significantly less likely to die from cardiovascular disease, infection or respiratory (lung and airways) disease. Moreover they were 22% less likely to die from any cause compared with people who had a lower quantity of fibre in their diet (10-13g per day). Thus it seems that a high fibre diet carries a number of health benefits besides reducing the risk of bowel cancer.

'Fibre seems to help prevent the growth of polyps and also their transformation into cancer.'

Lifestyle

Alcohol

As mentioned in chapter 1, even small amounts of alcohol (below the recommended daily number of units for men and women) are associated with a higher risk of developing bowel cancer. The risk is also higher for ex-drinkers. The message here is to enjoy alcohol sensibly, in moderation and to have a healthy diet.

Smoking

There is a clear link between smoking and the risk of getting bowel cancer, apart from all the other health-related issues associated with smoking. As with alcohol, even ex-smokers have a higher risk compared with people who have never smoked.

Research shows that stopping smoking carries some of the biggest possible benefits in health improvement, and that most heavy smokers want to quit but are unable to do so. For many, smoking is an addiction that seems impossible to break however there are numerous NHS Stop Smoking services available locally that can provide you with continued support and treatment to help you quit, or at the very least, to cut down.

Exercise

People who do not exercise have a higher risk of getting bowel cancer. The government recognises that modern lifestyles are different in that fewer people take regular exercise and this coincides with an increase in obesity in the general population.

Regular physical activity not only reduces the risk of getting diseases such as cancer, diabetes and cardiovascular disease, but it makes people feel better, keeps the body in good condition and promotes longer life.

The recommended level activity for adults is for 30 minutes of moderate exercise (such as walking) at least five days a week. However, being realistic, lifestyle changes are often the most difficult to make, especially if you are trying to change your lifestyle on your own. As with all lifestyle changes, gradual changes are best, so as far as exercising is concerned, it is best to start gradually and work up, especially for those who do not exercise at all. Making changes to your lifestyle, such as taking exercise or increasing your current level of exercise, is often much easier if you are part of a group of like-minded individuals, so working with family and/or friends allows you to motivate and guide each other, increasing the chances of success.

Walking, jogging, cycling and swimming are all exercises which are effective in giving your whole body a workout. The NHS Change4Life website contains very useful information about exercise and finding local exercise activities in your area (further details are provided in the help list).

Maintaining a healthy weight

I have already mentioned that there is a strong link between obesity and an increased risk of bowel cancer. Maintaining a healthy weight will reduce your risk if you are overweight or obese. The BMI is a good guide to your healthy weight range and you should aim for a BMI of no more than 25 if your build allows it. Losing weight is a lifestyle change and requires dedication and perseverance but the health benefits are substantial. The best way to lose weight is to combine regular exercise with a healthy balanced diet. Support .from your family and friends is invaluable, as are organisations such as Weight Loss Resources (www.weightlossresources.co.uk) and WeightWatchers (www.weightwatchers.co.uk), where you can join others who all have the same goal in mind.

Medical treatments

Aspirin

A recent clinical study has shown that taking aspirin reduces the risk of dying from bowel cancer by 35% and the incidence of bowel cancer was reduced by 24% over 20 years with daily doses of aspirin of (75–300 mg). The study involved more than 14,000 patients with bowel cancer. However, taking aspirin over the long term can increase the risk of stomach ulcers and bleeding in the bowel, so a decision as to whether aspirin would be of benefit would be dependent upon the opinion of the doctor and whether people have an increased risk of bowel cancer, such as those with FAP, ulcerative colitis or Crohn's disease. With the benefits of colonoscopy and sigmoidoscopy to screen for bowel cancer, this is an appropriate time to discuss starting on aspirin. If you are otherwise healthy and you have no obvious risk of bowel cancer it is not advisable to take any form of preventative medicine without at least discussing it with your doctor.

Summing Up

- If you are invited to a screening for bowel cancer then it is very important to attend. Early diagnosis of bowel cancer through screening has been proven to save lives.

- There are a number of risk factors associated with bowel cancer that can be modified to reduce the risk of getting the disease:

- Eat a healthy and balanced diet which includes plenty of fresh fruit and vegetables, lean protein (such as white meat and fish).

- Try to include plenty of fibre (at least 18g per day) in your diet.

- Aim to eat no more than 70g of red meat per day.

- Stick to the guideline daily amounts for calories, protein, carbohydrate, sugars, fat, saturates, fibre and salt.

- Take regular exercise and maintain a healthy weight for your height.

- Enjoy alcohol in moderation and if you are a smoker then try to quit or at least cut down.

- For those people who are at higher risk of bowel cancer, a doctor may recommend a medical treatment such as aspirin.

Chapter Three

Symptoms of Bowel Cancer

What are the symptoms of bowel cancer?

Many of the symptoms of bowel cancer are vague and are shared with other conditions such as haemorrhoids and inflammatory bowel disease. The symptoms of bowel cancer can also differ depending on where the cancer is located. Here are some of the symptoms of bowel cancer:

- Bleeding from the rectum or blood in the stools (can be bright red in cancer of the rectum or dark brown/black if the tumour is further up the bowel). Spots of bright red blood on the toilet paper is also a common sign of haemorrhoids.

- A prolonged change in your regular bowel habits (for example diarrhoea or the stools becoming noticeably softer).

- Pain in the abdomen (the main symptom in cancer of the ascending colon) or rectum.

- Tenesmus (a straining sensation in the rectum, sometimes painful, that feels like wanting to go to the toilet but you are unable to pass any stools).

- A lump in your lower abdomen that can be felt by the doctor.

- Weight loss.

- A feeling of being constantly tired or short of breath (often as a result of blood loss from your bowels).

'The symptoms of bowel cancer are vague and shared with other less serious conditions.'

If the level of blood loss is high you may develop a condition known as anaemia, where the number of red blood cells in your body that carry blood to your tissues decreases, leaving you feeling very tired and breathless. Occasionally a tumour can cause an obstruction in the bowel, leading to prolonged pain in the abdomen, constipation and feelings of being bloated or sick.

When to see a doctor

'If there is any lasting change in your bowel habits . . . you must see your GP urgently. You will not be wasting your GP's time and the earlier bowel cancer is diagnosed, the better the treatment and the outcome.'

The symptoms of bowel cancer are shared by many other conditions such as piles (or haemorrhoids) which cause bleeding from the rectum or inflammatory bowel diseases such as ulcerative colitis and Crohn's disease. However, the symptoms of bowel cancer are not obvious and some people will not have any symptoms. Talking about bowel problems or going to the toilet can be intensely embarrassing and therefore we prefer to keep bowel problems to ourselves.

However, if there is any lasting change in your bowel habits (such as prolonged diarrhoea or softer stools than normal that lasts for a week or more) or any persistent pain in your abdomen, you must see your GP urgently. Most people find that they have a temporary condition or an illness than can be managed and that is less serious than cancer. You will not be wasting your GP's time and the earlier bowel cancer is diagnosed, the better the treatment and the outcome.

Seeing a specialist

The NICE guidelines

Because the symptoms of bowel cancer are shared by many other less serious conditions, it can be difficult for your GP to decide whether to refer you to a specialist. In many cases, your GP might ask you to wait first to see if your symptoms improve or respond to treatment such as antibiotics if an infection is suspected.

The National Institute for Health and Clinical Excellence (NICE) is a government body of experts that issues guidance on how specific diseases should be diagnosed and managed by the NHS. NICE has issued guidance on the treatment of bowel cancer in order to help GPs decide which patients to refer to a specialist. The guidance states that people with symptoms that are listed in the guidance should be sent to a specialist within two weeks of visiting their family doctor. This is called an urgent referral.

Urgent referrals

The NICE guidance states that you should see a specialist within two weeks of seeing your GP if you are:

- Aged 60 years and older, with bleeding from the rectum for six weeks or longer, or with a change in bowel habit to looser or more frequent stools continuing for six weeks or longer.

- Aged 40 to 59 years and have bleeding from the rectum with either a change of bowel habit towards looser stools or more frequent stools for six weeks or longer.

- Any age and have a lump in your abdomen in the area of your large bowel (colon or rectum).

The guidance states that unexplained anaemia could be due to bleeding from a bowel cancer and advises GPs to refer people with unexplained anaemia for tests. The guidance also points out that people who have the following symptoms, but do not have any lump in the abdomen, are very unlikely to have cancer:

- Bleeding from the back passage, with soreness, itching and pain.

- A change in normal bowel habits to harder, less frequent stools.

- Pain in the abdomen without any sign that there is a blockage of the bowel.

Summing Up

- The symptoms of bowel cancer are vague and shared with other less serious conditions.

- Early diagnosis of bowel cancer is critical to ensure the best possible outcome.

- The important thing to remember is to see your GP urgently if there is any lasting change in your bowel habits, a prolonged pain or anything else out of the ordinary.

- Don't be embarrassed to see a doctor – they will deal with these problems on a daily basis and it could save your life.

- If you are considered to be at risk, your GP will refer you to a specialist.

Chapter Four

Diagnosis of Bowel Cancer

As I mentioned earlier, early diagnosis is critical for the best possible outcome in bowel cancer; the earlier the diagnosis the better the outcome and those cancers that are diagnosed very early can be cured with surgery. Diagnosis of bowel cancer is becoming more accurate and sophisticated and this chapter summarises the main methods by which bowel cancer can be diagnosed.

'Early diagnosis is critical for the best possible outcome in bowel cancer; the earlier the diagnosis the better the outcome.'

Diagnostic techniques

Endoscopy (colonoscopy and sigmoidoscopy)

Bowel cancer is usually diagnosed during a colonoscopy or sigmoidoscopy, where a small sample of tissue (biopsy) is taken from any polyps that are seen during the procedure. The biopsy is analysed in a laboratory for the presence of any cancer cells. Colonoscopy and sigmoidoscopy procedures are explained in chapter 2.

Virtual colonoscopy

Other techniques for diagnosing bowel cancer are also used. A 'virtual colonoscopy' can be performed. This procedure uses CT (computerised tomography) scanning. The CT scanner takes a series of X-ray images of the body which are processed by a computer to produce image 'slices' through the body or even three-dimensional images. The virtual colonoscopy technique can show the presence of polyps or other unusual or abnormal changes to the bowel and pinpoint their exact location. Preparation for the procedure usually involves taking a laxative and an enema to make sure the rectum is empty of stools. A small tube is placed into the rectum to pump in air to make it easier to obtain images of the large bowel.

The advantage of virtual colonoscopy (also known as computerised tomography colonography or CTC) is that it is an easier and more comfortable procedure than colonoscopy or sigmoidoscopy as it does not use an endoscope and is a short procedure (usually about ten minutes). Unlike colonoscopy and sigmoidoscopy you do not need to be given a drug to make you relax (sedative). This means that you can return home or continue with your usual daily activities without having to rely on another person to assist you. Virtual colonoscopy looks at the whole of the abdomen and not just the lining of the bowel so it can be useful for showing any tumours that might have formed outside the bowel. Unfortunately, it cannot be used to take biopsies.

Magnetic resonance imaging

Magnetic resonance imaging (MRI) is a scanning procedure similar to CT scanning, but uses a machine that generates a very powerful magnetic field. The images obtained using this procedure can be highly detailed and it may allow tumours to be more easily seen than with other techniques. MRI can be used to accurately determine how far a tumour has spread within the bowel wall or to look for the presence of metastases in the liver.

Ultrasound

This technique uses sound waves that are sent through the body from a probe. The probe picks up the reflected sound from organs and structures within the body and displays them on a monitor. In endoscopic ultrasound (EUS) the technique is combined with an endoscope and can be used to examine the lining of the rectum and colon and to help to stage any cancer found there (see section on staging opposite).

Barium enema

The bowel contains air and this means that normal X-rays will not show enough detail. Barium is a solution that is given to coat the lining of the bowel like a paint. It allows the lining to show up clearly as white areas on an X-ray. A barium enema requires the bowel to be completely clear of any faeces and so preparation involves strong laxatives. You will also be asked not to eat any food for 24 hours and to drink only water.

Differential diagnosis

There are a number of other conditions which share the same symptoms as those of bowel cancer and it is important to rule these out before the diagnosis of cancer is made. The process of ruling out other conditions is called differential diagnosis and involves the doctor looking at the symptoms and determining which condition most closely matches these to help make a diagnosis.

Staging of bowel cancer

Like many other cancers, bowel cancer is 'staged'. The process of staging allows the doctor to determine how large the cancer is, whether it has spread, and if so, by how much. There are two staging systems that are used to stage bowel cancer.

'The process of staging allows the doctor to determine how large the cancer is, whether it has spread, and if so, by how much.'

Dukes staging system

The Dukes staging system was created by a British doctor called Cuthbert Dukes in 1932 for classifying colorectal cancer. The Dukes system has four stages: A, B, C and D. These were adapted in 1954 to add sub-divisions to stages B and C. The full staging system is summarised in the table overleaf.

Dukes Stage	Description
A	The tumour is confined to the lining of the bowel
B1	The tumour has grown into the muscle wall of the bowel but not beyond it
B2	The tumour has grown beyond the muscle wall of the bowel, but there is no lymph node involvement
C1	The tumour has grown into the muscle wall of the bowel but not beyond it. Lymph nodes are involved
C2	The tumour has grown beyond the muscle wall of the bowel and lymph nodes are also involved
D	The tumour has spread to other parts of the body (metastasis)

Dukes staging system for bowel cancer

TNM staging system

The TNM (tumour, node, metastases) staging system is widely used for staging different types of cancer and is taking over from the Dukes system for staging bowel cancer.

T describes the tumour size and whether it has spread and is subdivided into T1, T2, T3 or T4 according to size:

- T1 – The tumour is confined to the lining of the bowel.

- T2 – The tumour has grown into the muscle wall of the bowel.

- T3 – The tumour has grown into the outermost layer of the bowel (the peritoneum) or into other organs or structures adjoining the bowel.

- T4 – The tumour has grown into other areas of the bowel, other organs or structures adjoining the bowel, or has grown beyond the peritoneum.

The T stages are summarised opposite.

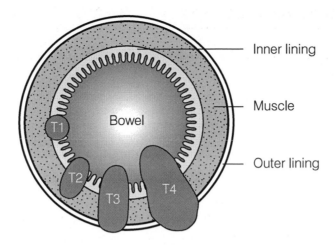

Inner lining

Muscle

Outer lining

T stages of bowel cancer

N describes the involvement of any lymph nodes and is subdivided into N1, N2 and N3 according to whether or not cancer cells are present in lymph nodes and if they are, how many lymph nodes are involved:

- N0 – There are no cancer cells in the lymph nodes close to the bowel.

- N1 – Between one and three lymph nodes close to the bowel contain cancer cells

- N2 – There are either four or more lymph nodes at least 3cm away from the bowel that contain cancer cells or the lymph nodes that are close to the main blood vessels that surround the bowel contain cancer cells.

M describes metastases and is subdivided into M0 and M1:

- M0 – The tumour has not spread outside the bowel to other parts of the body.

- M1 – The tumour has spread to other parts of the body such as the liver.

When describing the stage of cancer using the TNM system, the T, N and M elements are combined to show how advanced or otherwise the cancer is, for example T1, N0, M0 would describe a tumour that is confined to the lining of the bowel (T1), there are no cancer cells in the lymph nodes (N0) and it has not spread to any other part of the body (M0). There are 5 stages for bowel cancer (0,1, 2, 3 and 4) and these are summarised in the table overleaf.

Stage	Description	TNM Classification
0	Carcinoma in situ (CIS) – the tumour is confined to the lining of the bowel	T0, TIS (Tumour in situ)
1	The tumour has grown into the lining of the bowel (T1) or has grown into the muscle wall (T2)	T1, N0, M0 or T2, N0, M0
2a	The tumour has grown through the peritoneum (T3) but has not spread to the lymph nodes or other parts of the body	T3, N0, M0
2b	The tumour has grown through the peritoneum and into other areas of the bowel or other organs or structures adjoining the bowel (T4) but has not spread to the lymph nodes or other parts of the body	T4, N0, M0
3a	The tumour has grown into the lining of the bowel (T1) or has grown into the muscle wall (T2) between one and three close lymph nodes have cancer cells in them	T1, N1, M0 or T2, N1, M0
3b	The tumour has grown through the peritoneum and into other areas of the bowel or other organs or structures adjoining the bowel (T4) and between one and three close lymph nodes have cancer cells in them	T3, N1, M0 or T4, N1, M0
3c	The tumour can be of any size (any T) and four or more close lymph nodes have cancer cells in them	T (any), N2, M0
4	The cancer has spread to other parts of the body such as the liver or lungs through either the bloodstream or the lymphatic system	T (any), N (any), M1

The five TNM stages of bowel cancer

The TNM staging system may seem complicated but it has been designed to ensure the most accurate description of the stage of bowel cancer. This in turn allows the doctor to plan the most appropriate treatment.

Biopsy

The term 'biopsy' refers to a sample of tissue that is taken for analysis. In bowel cancer the biopsy tissue can be from the tumour or polyp or a nearby lymph node. A tumour or polyp biopsy is usually taken during a colonoscopy or sigmoidoscopy using a special surgical tool contained within the endoscope.

Since lymph nodes are located outside the bowel a different technique is required. A biopsy can be taken using a fine needle inserted into the lymph node under local anaesthetic (needle biopsy). However the needle biopsy only provides a small amount of tissue and this might not be enough for analysis of bowel cancer. Alternatively, an open biopsy procedure may be used, where a small cut (incision) is made under local anaesthetic and the sample of lymph node is surgically removed. Finally, there is a special technique called sentinal lymph node biopsy, that is often used in cancer and this technique allows the doctor to find the best lymph node from which to take a biopsy. A small amount of dye is injected into the tumour, which flows into the first (sentinal) lymph node into which the cancer cells would spread. The biopsy would be taken from the sentinal and perhaps one or two neighbouring lymph nodes.

Once the biopsy samples are obtained they are sent to a laboratory where the samples are viewed under a microscope to test for the presence of cancer cells.

Summing Up

- Early diagnosis is critical for the best possible outcome in bowel cancer; the earlier the diagnosis the better the outcome.

- Diagnostic techniques for bowel cancer include:

    Endoscopy (colonoscopy and sigmoidoscopy)

    Magnetic resonance imaging

    Ultrasound

    Barium enema

- Bowel cancer is 'staged' to allow the doctor to determine the best treatment approach. There are two staging systems for bowel cancer:

    Dukes (being phased out)

    TNM

- A biopsy is a sample of tissue taken to be tested for the presence of cancer cells.

Chapter Five

Treating Bowel Cancer

How your bowel cancer is treated depends upon how advanced it is (what stage it is at). Once the cancer has been staged the doctor can then plan the best course of treatment. There are three main options for treating bowel cancer: surgery, radiotherapy and chemotherapy. These techniques can be used individually but are more commonly used sequentially (one after the other) for example surgery can be followed by chemotherapy to reduce the likelihood of the cancer recurring or cancer cells spreading to other parts of the body. These treatments can also be given in combination with each other, for example radiotherapy is often given at the same time as chemotherapy and is known as chemoradiotherapy or chemoradiation. Combining different treatments often makes them more effective against the cancer cells.

Surgery

Surgery is the most effective treatment for bowel cancer and can be curative for tumours that have not spread. About 80% of bowel tumours can be removed using surgery. A surgeon removes (resects) the tumour and an area of healthy tissue surrounding the tumour (margin) to ensure that all of the cancer cells are removed. With very small tumours surgery alone may be sufficient followed by regular follow-up visits to make sure that the cancer has gone. Unfortunately, most bowel cancers are more advanced and larger than this.

When the tumour has grown beyond a certain size, surgery may still be possible but would involve the removal of a significant part of the bowel which would interfere with the normal function of the bowel and requires a stoma. (see chapter 6).

'Surgery is the most effective treatment for bowel cancer and can be curative for tumours that have not spread. About 80% of bowel tumours can be removed using surgery.'

If the tumour is too large or has grown into, or spread to, other parts of the body, the surgeon may not be able to remove it completely without risking serious complications such as bleeding. In this situation the surgeon might remove part of the tumour (debulking) and treatment may also include chemotherapy and radiotherapy to shrink the remaining tumour or keep it under control. Any treatment that is given after the primary treatment (in this case surgery) is known as adjuvant treatment. It may then be possible to remove the remaining tumour after it has shrunk. Alternatively, chemotherapy or radiotherapy may be given before surgery (known as neoadjuvant treatment) to shrink the tumour so that the surgeon can remove all of the cancer.

In very advanced cancer, the tumour might be considered inoperable. In other words, surgery would not be appropriate as the tumour is so large or has invaded so many other organs and tissues that the risk to the patient is considered to be too high when weighed against the benefits. In this case the aim of treatment would be not to try to cure the cancer but to control it for as long as possible and give the patient the best possible care for the rest of their life.

Surgery offers the best chance of a cure for bowel cancer if all of the tumour can be removed. Though the majority of people who have bowel cancer are offered surgery, not all can be cured as the disease may have spread to the lymph nodes or may have metastasised. If this is the case, further treatment such as adjuvant chemotherapy may be needed after surgery.

Types of surgery for bowel cancer

Local resection

If the tumour is very small and has not spread beyond the lining of the bowel, then it can be removed, together with a small margin of healthy tissue, in a procedure known as a local resection. This can be carried out using a cutting tool attached to an endoscope. In rectal cancer, local resection is known as a transanal resection.

Colectomy

Surgery to remove part of the colon that is affected by cancer is known as colectomy. If a section of colon is removed from the left side, the procedure is known as a left hemicolectomy. If a section of colon is removed from the right side, the procedure is known as a right hemicolectomy. An operation to remove part of the transverse colon is called a transverse colectomy. In sigmoid colectomy the sigmoid colon is removed whilst removal of the entire colon is known as a total colectomy.

When the cancer-bearing tissue has been removed, the surgeon will rejoin the two healthy ends of the bowel in a procedure called an anastamosis. This may be done straight away but often it may be necessary to allow some time for the bowel to heal, and in this case the surgeon may fit a temporary stoma, or opening in the body wall that the bowel is stitched to in order to allow food waste to be collected outside the body in a stoma bag (See illustration below). When the damaged area of bowel has healed sufficiently, the temporary stoma will be reversed and the two ends of bowel will be rejoined. In the case of a total colectomy the lower part of the small bowel (ileum) may need to be used to create a stoma (ileostomy) and in some cases this can be permanent.

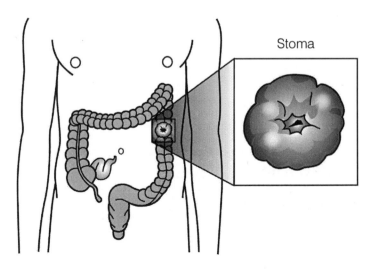

Stoma

Stoma (colostomy)

Total mesenteric excision (TME)

In rectal cancer, the mesentery is routinely removed at the same time as the tumour and a margin of healthy tissue. This is because the mesentery contains lymph nodes and any cancer cells that spread are likely to be found in them. Surgery for rectal cancer may require a temporary stoma. If the entire rectum needs to be removed, then a permanent stoma will be needed.

Chemotherapy

'Chemotherapy drugs have a number of side effects because they affect all dividing cells. It is important to remember that side effects of chemotherapy are temporary and will disappear after chemotherapy is finished.'

Chemotherapy refers to the use of drugs to treat cancer. There are a wide variety of anticancer drugs and they work in different ways. On most occasions they are given in combination, with a range of drugs that have different modes of action being used together. This approach improves the likelihood of response.

Most chemotherapy drugs work systemically (throughout the entire body) and they do not attack just the cancer cells but healthy cells as well. As a result, all anticancer drugs have a number of side effects because they affect all dividing cells.

Side effects of chemotherapy

Since chemotherapy drugs affect all cells, not just the cancer cells, especially those that are dividing rapidly such as hair, skin and cells lining the GI tract and bone marrow, these sites are where side effects will be most noticeable.

It is important to remember that side effects of chemotherapy are temporary and will disappear after chemotherapy is finished.

Nausea and vomiting

All chemotherapy drugs cause some amount of nausea (feeling sick) and vomiting (being sick). Because of this fact it is common practice for you to be given a drug to stop you being sick (an anti-emetic) at the same time as you start your chemotherapy. The most commonly used drug for bowel cancer, 5-FU, causes a moderate amount of nausea and this can usually be easily controlled with anti-emetics.

Mucositis

This is soreness and inflammation of the lining of the mouth, sometimes with ulcers. It can be difficult to eat, drink or swallow if you have mucositis, although you can be given painkillers if it is a real problem or antiseptic mouthwashes if you have ulcers and they become infected.

Diarrhoea

This is also a very common problem with chemotherapy drugs. It is caused by healthy cells in the bowel being damaged by the treatment. As a result they do not absorb nutrients and water from the food as they should and the stools are very watery. One risk of prolonged or severe diarrhoea is dehydration (fluid loss) as the water is not being absorbed from your food, and in these cases you can be given treatments to help stop the diarrhoea and to replace lost fluids

Hair loss (alopecia)

It is not uncommon for people having chemotherapy to experience hair loss or thinning. The amount of hair lost varies depending on which chemotherapy drugs are used, and also varies from person to person. Whilst some people may lose very little hair, others will lose most if not all of their hair. As chemotherapy progresses those that do lose a significant amount of hair tend to lose it in clumps. This can be especially devastating for some. There is specialist help and support available through the NHS (counselling, advice and temporary hair pieces and wigs). However, as with most of the side effects of chemotherapy, hair will almost always grow back after chemotherapy has finished.

Suppression of the bone marrow

The central part of many of our bones, such as the leg bones, hip bone and breastbone (sternum) contain bone marrow, where the red blood cells (those that carry oxygen to our tissues through arteries and veins), platelets (the cells that help blood to clot when we injure ourselves) and white cells (those that make up our immune system and fight infection) are made. The bone marrow is highly active, with millions of red cells, white cells and platelets being released into the blood every second and it is often affected by chemotherapy drugs. What usually happens is that chemotherapy kills many of the bone marrow cells, reducing the number of cells the bone marrow is able to produce, a process known as bone marrow suppression. This can result in a reduced ability to fight infections as white cell numbers drop, problems with blood not clotting properly after injury or spontaneous bleeding (nose bleeds are common) as platelet counts drop, or anaemia and tiredness as the number of red cells being produced by the bone marrow falls.

If you are suffering from infections you may be given antibiotics to treat this. Most people have lowered levels of white cells during chemotherapy, but if the counts are very low then there are drugs that can boost white cell production or transfusions of white cells can be given. Similarly, if bleeding problems become serious, platelet transfusions can help restore the platelet counts towards normal, and anaemia (resulting from a low red cell count) can be treated with a blood transfusion or blood boosting drugs if necessary.

Commonly used chemotherapy drugs in bowel cancer

5-fluorouracil (5-FU)

This drug has been used to treat advanced bowel cancer for more than 25 years. 5-fluorouracil is similar to one of the components of DNA, uracil, but with a slightly different structure. When the DNA of cancer cells is copied as they divide, 5-FU interferes with this process and helps to prevent the cancer cells from producing new DNA. As a result the drug helps to stop cancer cells from dividing. 5-FU is usually given through a large blood vessel, directly into the bloodstream, either as an injection of a single large dose (bolus) or by introducing the drug more gradually through a drip or using a pump over several hours or longer (infusion). 5-FU is given in combination with folinic acid (see opposite).

5-FU can be given by infusion into the hepatic portal vein (the main vein that carries blood to the liver from the bowel) for treating liver metastases. Using this method a high dose of the drug can be delivered to the tumours in the liver.

5-FU is considered to be a mild treatment with few side effects and most people cope well with it, although some will develop nausea/vomiting, mucositis, diarrhoea and bone marrow suppression. A hand-foot syndrome known as palmar-plantar erythema can occur in people who are given the drug by infusion. It causes reddening, soreness and peeling of the skin on the hands and feet and can be quite frightening, although it is not usually serious for most people and they can carry on with their treatment. If it is a problem, then the doctor can choose to delay treatment until the condition clears up.

Folinic acid

Folinic acid (also known as leucovorin) makes 5-FU more effective and the two drugs are given in combination for this reason. The combination of 5-FU and folinic acid is easy to give, whether by intravenous bolus or infusion and various dosages of both drugs have been used over various time periods. A planned course of chemotherapy given over time is known as a regimen. One such regimen of 5-FU and folinic acid is the de Gramont regimen, which combines both infusion and bolus doses of 5-FU with high dose folinic acid, and is very effective in metastatic disease. Different doses of 5-FU are given at different times of a treatment period. The dose of many chemotherapy drugs is calculated according to body surface area in square metres (m^2):

200 mg/m^2 folinic acid as a 2-hour infusion on days 1 and 2 of a two week cycle:

- 5-FU 400mg/m^2 as intravenous (i.v.) bolus on days 1 and 2

- 5-FU 600mg/m^2 as an infusion over 22 hours on days 1 and 2

This is normally repeated every 2 weeks.

Oxaliplatin

Oxaliplatin is a drug based on the precious metal platinum and it interferes with the production of DNA, inhibiting cancer cell division and replication. It is very active in colorectal cancer and when used in combination with the de Gramont regimen of 5-FU and folinic acid it improves the effectiveness, doubling the response rate.

Oxaliplatin is a well-tolerated platinum-based drug (many drugs in this class, especially cisplatin, are highly toxic). The commonest side effects are nausea, bone marrow suppression and sensory peripheral neuropathy, a condition which affects the nerves causing tingling and numbness in the hands and feet. In most people this side effect is mild but in some it can become a real problem and since it is related to the dose of oxaliplatin, the doctor will often reduce the dose of the drug to see if the condition improves.

Irinotecan

This drug stops the DNA from unwinding during cell division so that it cannot copy itself. As a result, the cancer cells cannot replicate. Irinotecan inhibits an enzyme called topoisomerase 1, which unzips the DNA structure. It is usually given by intravenous infusion in combination with other chemotherapy drugs such as 5-FU and folinic acid.

Irinotecan is a powerful drug and its side effects include nausea/vomiting, delayed onset diarrhoea which can be serious and need prompt treatment, bone marrow suppression and hair loss.

Capecitabine

Capecitabine is an example of a prodrug, in other words one that is inactive and only converted into an active form when it is inside the body or inside the tumour. Prodrugs tend to be more selective for their target. It means that capecitabine is converted into its active form, fluorouracil (5-FU) when it is inside the tumour, and there is a markedly lower chance of it attacking healthy, non-cancerous cells, which helps to reduce side effects. Another advantage of capecitabine is that it can be taken by mouth (oral) rather than being injected (the case for most chemotherapy drugs used to treat bowel cancer).

Capecitabine can be given with uracil and folinic acid as first-line (initial) chemotherapy treatment for metastatic bowel cancer or as adjuvant treatment (combined with oxaliplatin) following surgery in advanced (TNM stage 3 or Dukes C) bowel cancer.

Capecitabine has similar side effects to 5-FU as the drugs are very similar.

Tegafur

Like capecitabine, tegafur is also a prodrug of fluorouracil. It is given as a tablet with uracil (which helps to stop the breakdown of the active part of tegafur, fluorouracil) and folinic acid as first-line treatment of metastatic bowel cancer.

Tegafur has similar side effects to 5-FU and capecitabine as the drugs are very similar.

Receiving your chemotherapy

Chemotherapy drugs are very powerful and for this reason your treatment will need to be started in hospital, many of which have a specialist chemotherapy unit. The treatment will be given by specially trained cancer doctors (oncologists) and/or nurses. Most chemotherapy drugs will be delivered through a blood vessel, which will involve putting a needle into a vein, usually one in the arm, although a larger vein inside your chest can also be used (sometimes known as putting in a central line). In most cases you will be asked to remain in the chemotherapy unit while you are having the treatment, allowing the doctors and nurses to make sure that everything is happening as it should. Some chemotherapy drugs are given as rapid injections (bolus) and others, such as capecitabine, are given as tablets or capsules, so you may be allowed to go home earlier with these types of treatment. Once started, some treatments can be given at home and in this case a doctor or nurse will visit to give the treatment.

Chemotherapy drugs are given as a treatment course, which usually consists of a series of cycles, often with a rest between each cycle to allow the body to recover before the next cycle starts. For example, a common cycle of treatment is 28 days, with a rest period of seven days. Courses of chemotherapy are usually 4-6 cycles long, although they may be longer than this, so you will need to go to the hospital regularly to have your treatment.

Radiotherapy

This technique involves pointing a high intensity beam of radioactive particles directly at the tumour in order to kill the cancer cells. Modern radiotherapy machines are able to focus the beam of particles to the exact size and shape of the tumour, which limits the damage to surrounding healthy cells and the tissue that the particles have to travel through to reach the tumour. Radiotherapy that is delivered to the body from outside as a beam of particles is called external beam radiotherapy.

Radiotherapy is usually used to treat rectal cancer and is normally given in addition to other treatments. For example, radiotherapy can be given ahead of surgery (preoperatively, neoadjuvant treatment) to shrink the tumour, making it easier to remove, and chemotherapy drugs such as 5-FU are often given at the same time as they make cancer cells more sensitive to the effects of radiotherapy. If your tumour is large and difficult to remove using surgery, you may be given radiotherapy after surgery (postoperatively, adjuvant treatment) to help destroy any cancer cells left behind or if there are cancer cells in the lymph nodes.

'Radiotherapy is usually used to treat rectal cancer and is normally given in addition to other treatments.'

In addition, a newer internal radiotherapy treatment called brachytherapy is available, where the radioactive particles are contained inside a tube and delivered inside the body. With rectal cancer the brachytherapy tube is inserted through the anus into the rectum and placed close to the tumour, where it will be left in place to help shrink the tumour so that it can be removed surgically.

Radiotherapy is usually given at regular intervals for about five weeks, although the time may be longer or shorter than this. External beam radiotherapy is planned using a machine called a simulator, which does not produce any radiotherapy, but takes X-rays and moves in exactly the same way as the radiotherapy machine will move during actual treatment. The doctor will use these X-rays and also CT scans where required, to determine the size and shape of the tumour and how much radiotherapy to use. The radiographer or doctor will draw a series of marks on the skin to allow the radiotherapy machine to deliver the treatment to exactly the right place. Once the planning is finished you can then receive your radiotherapy for real. The treatment is given in fractions (in other words little and often) as this seems to be most effective and patients cope better with smaller amounts of treatment given at regular intervals. Typically, a course of radiotherapy would involve daily treatments during the week (Monday to Friday) with no treatment at the weekend (a rest period) but, alternatively, you could be asked to have radiotherapy daily without a break.

Side effects of radiotherapy

Though radiotherapy is very precise in treating only tumour tissue, there are side effects caused by the radiation beam passing through normal tissue to reach the tumour. Every person who is treated with radiotherapy will tolerate it differently; some may experience no side effects at all, whereas others might develop side effects that make them feel physically ill or interfere with their normal daily activities. The side effects of radiotherapy are also dependent upon the location of the tumour and whether any other organs or structures are affected (such as the spinal cord, liver or kidneys). Radiotherapy side effects are usually divided into those that appear while radiotherapy is being given (early effects) or those that may develop some time after the course of treatment has finished (late effects).

Early effects

These can be generalised, such as feeling tired and lethargic during treatment, becoming anxious or depressed due to repeatedly going to the hospital to have treatment, or they can be as a result of the radiation damaging normal cells. In bowel cancer, radiotherapy can damage the skin in the path of the beam, causing reddening, soreness, rashes or flaking. Diarrhoea is a common problem as the normal function of the non-cancerous bowel is disrupted. Early effects relate to the interference with the function of normal cells by radiotherapy but once the treatment has finished and these cells repair themselves, the early effects will eventually disappear.

Late effects

Late effects are more serious than early effects of radiotherapy as they are often the result of a permanent change in otherwise normal cells and tissues caused by exposure to radiotherapy. Late effects appear many months after radiotherapy has finished and may include fibrosis (thickening and hardening) of skin or bleeding and holes (perforation) appearing in affected bowel tissue. Fortunately, late effects of radiotherapy are rare and most people will not experience them.

Summing Up

- The treatment of bowel cancer is dependent upon what stage the cancer is at when it is diagnosed.

- The main treatment for bowel cancer is surgery and it offers the best chance of cure.

- Other treatments include chemotherapy and radiotherapy, which can be given before (neoadjuvant), during or after surgery (adjuvant) to make the treatment of the disease as effective as possible.

- Chemotherapy and radiotherapy affect healthy cells too and are associated with a number of side effects, though these will eventually disappear after treatment stops.

Chapter Six

Living with Bowel Cancer

Dealing with the diagnosis

For most people, being told by a doctor that you have cancer can be shocking and devastating. You may feel as if your whole world has been turned inside out and that you have no control over your life anymore. You may feel alone and afraid. However, cancer is such a serious and potentially life-changing event that you should not have to deal with it on your own. Talking to your friends and family about your diagnosis is very important – people are very supportive when they learn that a friend or a loved one has cancer.

For many, the diagnosis of cancer is too much to take in and sometimes the reaction is one of disbelief or denial – 'it can't be true'. Some people decide to keep the news to themselves so as not to shock or worry others, but unfortunately cancer does not go away and a disease like this cannot be hidden forever.

One critical thing about receiving a diagnosis of bowel cancer is to be well informed about your disease. Cancer is now becoming a treatable long-term condition and many people with cancer will live active and normal lives. Those people who are well informed are able to make decisions about what to do and how to cope better with the consequences of their disease.

We all know somebody who either has or has had cancer so public awareness of the disease is very high and it is much less of a taboo subject than it once was. Talking to others about your disease will mean that it will be easier to cope with and you will get vital support. There are a number of bowel cancer organisations and support groups that can provide valuable support. Details of these organisations are given in the help list.

'One critical thing about receiving a diagnosis of bowel cancer is to be well informed about your disease . . . it is very important to put the disease into perspective . . . cancer is now evolving into a manageable long-term condition like diabetes, and people can now live with cancer for many years.'

Putting bowel cancer into perspective

We all know how shocking the word 'cancer' can be, particularly as for many people the diagnosis comes completely unexpectedly. However, it is very important to put the disease into perspective. Undoubtedly cancer still kills, but our vastly improved knowledge of this disease, coupled with new treatments and screening tests that improve early diagnosis, mean that cancer is now evolving into a manageable long-term condition like diabetes, and people can now live with cancer for many years.

There are also a number of popular misconceptions about bowel cancer and it is helpful to address these issues:

'I have just been diagnosed with bowel cancer. It will kill me won't it?'

Not necessarily. Cancer treatments have improved dramatically and many cases are being diagnosed earlier. The earlier cancer is diagnosed the earlier it can be treated and the better the outcome. In some cancers including bowel cancer, the disease can be cured if diagnosed very early. For those people who have not been diagnosed early, treatments are now so good that, even if your cancer cannot be cured you can live with the condition for many years and your life expectancy may not change that much.

'One of my parents or siblings has had bowel cancer. Does this mean I will get it too?'

Again, not necessarily. Whilst there are familial links to bowel cancer, most cases are not genetically linked and the cause is more often unknown, so if one of your first degree relatives has or has had the disease, it doesn't mean that everyone else in the family will get it or even be at greater risk of getting it. If more than one of your first degree relatives has or has had the disease, it may mean that there is a genetic link, but your doctor will be able find out for definite.

'Having bowel cancer means I won't be able to lead a normal life anymore.'

Absolutely not. Treatment for early disease can be curative and in this case it can be as if you never had the disease. If you require surgery, chemotherapy or radiotherapy alone or in combination, the treatment does not last forever and any problems you might experience with side effects will disappear with time, so while the treatment may interfere with your quality of life and activities of normal daily living, it won't be permanent. Even if you have a stoma as part of your treatment, these are very discreet and will not interfere with your daily activities. Most stomas are temporary and in these cases you will eventually have surgery to remove the stoma and rejoin the bowel, leaving just a small scar on your abdomen.

'Having had bowel cancer, I feel like half the person I was before.'

We all know that being diagnosed with cancer can be devastating and often changes the way you look at things forever. It is very common for people with cancer to give up any hope for the future and for the disease to destroy their confidence and self-esteem. Most people are very supportive once they find out that you have bowel cancer and nobody wants to have to go through life with cancer on their own. Nobody will think any less of you because you have or have had cancer. Support from others will lift your confidence, as will focussing on the positive things in your life (your family, friends, memories of happy times). Remaining active and aiming to live as normal a life as possible will help you to cope with any treatment you might need. Remember that surviving cancer is a monumental achievement and more and more people are surviving the disease. See the help list for organisations that can help and support you and your family.

'I have been told that my treatment has been successful and that there is no sign of the cancer. That must mean I'm cured, right?'

Be careful. A response to treatment can be defined in many different ways. True cure means that all of the cancer cells have been destroyed and the disease will not come back. Unfortunately, true cure is still relatively rare and most people who respond very well to treatment go into remission, which means that there is no evidence of any cancer cells. However, this does not necessarily mean that all of the cancer is gone, it means that no cancer cells can be detected. The reason I mention the difference between cure and remission is that I have heard people being told they are 'cured' of cancer only for it to come back many years later (a relapse), with devastating consequences.

I remember a young female work colleague of mine who had been treated for breast cancer with surgery. She was told after her operation that she was cured and didn't need any further treatment. Ten years later she began to get pain in her bones and was feeling continually tired. When she was examined by the local hospital, it was discovered that not only was she not cured, but the cancer had regrown and spread to her bones and liver. Within the next 18 months she had passed away from the disease and left a young family behind. In reality the cancer never really went away in her case and she was not actually cured but in remission and the cancer was still there but undetectable at the time she was told she was cured.

You must also remember that many cases of bowel cancer arise out of the blue with no obvious cause, and if the cause is still present after successful treatment the cancer can reappear at some point in the future.

If you are told that you are in complete remission, then it means that no evidence of cancer can be found. This is the best possible outcome for most people with cancer and in many cases signs of cancer will not reappear, but a complete remission is not the same as a cure. If your doctor has told you that you are cured of cancer then you have every right to ask exactly what this means as it can take a lot of time and repeated follow-up visits to determine whether you are cured or not.

'I have heard that some treatments for cancer such as radiotherapy and chemotherapy can themselves cause new cancers to develop, so isn't it dangerous to have these treatments for bowel cancer?'

Whilst it is true that some people may develop a second cancer (known as a secondary malignancy) after being treated with radiotherapy and/or chemotherapy, this is rare and it depends on the type of first cancer and the treatment. People with breast cancer, leukaemia and lymphoma as their primary cancer have developed secondary cancers many years after treatment of their original disease but the rate of secondary cancers is less than 5% in these people. These cancers are also often treated with much more aggressive chemotherapy than that used for bowel cancer, so the risk of getting a secondary cancer after treatment for bowel cancer is very low and the benefit of bowel cancer treatment far outweighs this risk.

Coping with bowel cancer after surgery

Surgery is a major procedure and requires time for recovery, and usually there will be pain and some blood loss afterwards. Removal of part of the bowel will usually mean that there will be a scar after the operation, especially after open surgery (where the surgeon has made a large incision in the abdomen). The scarring can be very visible and you may be very self-conscious of it, which can be embarrassing.

A new technique known as laparoscopic surgery (sometimes known as keyhole surgery) is being developed for the removal of bowel cancer. Instead of making a long open wound for traditional open surgery, the surgeon instead makes several small incisions (between 0.5 and 1.5 cm in length) and inserts a laparascope, which is a narrow tube, down which surgical instruments can be passed. The tumour can be cut out and removed through the tube. Whilst laparoscopic operations take longer than open surgery, the wounds are very small by comparison and many people who have laparoscopic operations have less pain afterwards and spend less time in hospital.

Analgesics will be given to help with pain and if the blood loss is significant you may have a blood transfusion or be given a blood boosting drug to stop you from suffering the tiredness of anaemia.

Coping with a stoma

For those who need to have a colostomy or ileostomy, a stoma is formed to allow the bowel contents to be emptied outside the body into a stoma bag (See illustration below). Having a colostomy can seem like a very distressing lifestyle change and can have a negative effect on your self-esteem, however it is important to remember that many colostomies are only temporary. People are quite often concerned that the bags will be visible to others or that they will smell, but in reality the stoma bags fit close to the body, are very discreet and most people will be unable to tell that you have a colostomy. Some people learn to flush out their colostomy several times a day and can fit a plug over the stoma instead of using a bag, which can help to build confidence.

'It is important to remember that many colostomies are only temporary.'

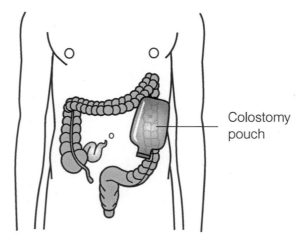

Colostomy pouch

Stoma fitted with colostomy bag

In addition there are trained stoma nurses who will help and support you in the hospital and at home. The nurse will provide you with help and education on how to look after your stoma and how to change the bags. The stoma nurse will also be readily contactable if you feel you need further help and support.

Emotional support and counselling

Emotional support

Having cancer creates a roller coaster of emotions: fear, anger, frustration, loneliness, despair to name but a few. If uncontrolled, these emotions can take over your life and they can have a very negative effect on your outlook for the future and your response to treatment.

It might be very hard to think positive if you have just been diagnosed with bowel cancer, but this is where emotional support and counselling can really help. Letting go of your emotions is one way of coping with the knowledge that you have cancer – there is nothing wrong with having a really good cry if that's what you feel you have to do to relieve some of the tension.

Whilst your immediate family and friends might be able to support you, they will not understand what you will be going through in the course of your disease. This is where talking to other bowel cancer patients can be really valuable. Many people who have survived bowel cancer have a real desire to give something back and help others with the disease. Patient Voices are a UK-based patient-to-patient network for people affected by bowel cancer and their relatives. They support others through their treatment, raise awareness of the disease and get involved in fundraising activities for medical research and charities. More information about Patient Voices can be found in the help list.

Counselling

You may not always feel comfortable talking about bowel cancer with your family and friends. They may be too close or too busy or they might worry too much about you once you have told them. Many people with bowel cancer feel isolated and alone and in these situations counselling and psychotherapy can be very valuable. Expressing your thoughts and feelings to a professional counsellor who doesn't know you can help you to understand your situation in a way that relatives and friends who know you would not be able to do. Counselling can give you back your hope and a sense of control if you are feeling distressed and powerless to do anything to help yourself.

'Expressing your thoughts and feelings to a professional counsellor who doesn't know you can help you to understand your situation in a way that relatives and friends who know you would not be able to do.'

Seeing a counsellor (seeing a 'shrink') is often thought of as a sign of weakness, but I can assure you from my own personal experience that counselling is anything but weak and it gives you the strength and clear direction to carry on after a traumatic or life-changing event.

Some years ago I was involved in a serious car crash where my car was hit from behind by another car at high speed on a dual carriageway as I slowed down to pull into a lay-by. My car was hit with such force that it left the road, careened down an embankment and ended up on its roof in a ditch. I was unconscious for several minutes but, remarkably, I was unhurt apart from some scratches and whiplash and was able to crawl out of the car through the back window. Whilst the physical trauma of the crash was minimal the psychological trauma was immense. For weeks afterwards I had recurrent flashbacks and nightmares about the crash and I was terrified of getting back in a car in case the same thing happened again, but I needed a car for my job as a sales rep, so I didn't feel I had any choice but to get back to driving. Fortunately, my employer was very supportive and provided counselling as well as a trained advanced driver to help me get back into the driving seat. The counsellor shared my experience and this was very valuable as my own family were too traumatised themselves to really offer me the support I needed. I also learned some relaxation techniques which stopped the flashbacks and nightmares. Counselling also gave me back the confidence to return to work and have since had more than 10 years of trouble-free driving.

Bowel cancer and working

For many working people with a diagnosis of bowel cancer, the ability to continue working during or after treatment is crucial, particularly if you happen to be the sole or main earner in your family. A recent change of government legislation offers protection for employees with cancer. The new Equality Act of 2010 prevents people with cancer from being discriminated against by their employer. This means that employers should not dismiss someone or make them redundant because, for example, they have had extended sick leave for treatment of their cancer, or are unable to do their job as well as before because of the symptoms associated with cancer or its treatment (for example fatigue). Employers also need to make reasonable allowances for employees with cancer, such as allowing time off to attend appointments, altering the job description or responsibilities to make things more acceptable for changing abilities, allowing a gradual return to work after a period of extended sick leave, or offering the opportunity to work from home if possible.

The Macmillan Cancer website has an excellent summary of the Equality Act (details for Macmillan can be found in the help list at the back of this book).

You may also be entitled to claim additional financial support from the government, such as Disability Living Allowance, regardless of whether you are working or not. More information on benefits can be found at the Directgov website (see help list).

Bowel cancer and quality of life

Quality of life is a measurement of how well we are able to do things and live our lives. We hardly ever think about quality of life until something happens that affects it in a negative way, often meaning that we can no longer do things as well as we could or cannot do them at all. Cancer and its treatment can have very profound negative effects on your quality of life. In fact, the negative effect that diseases such as cancer can have on quality of life is now so important that many clinical trials of new treatments for cancer will include questionnaires and surveys on quality of life to see how much of an effect the treatment has on activities of everyday life. In extreme cases, the effect of treatment of cancer on quality of life might be so bad that the negative effect on quality of life outweighs any benefit the treatment might deliver.

What this means for bowel cancer is that the disease may or may not affect your quality of life, but treatment will often make it noticeably worse. The impact that treatment has can be assessed using a simple tool known as the Linear Analogue Scale Assessment (LASA), a simple scale of 0-100 where 100 represents the best that you can be and 0 represents the worst that you can be (see overleaf). The scale is used for people to rate their energy level, ability to do daily activities and overall quality of life by marking the scale according to how they feel at the time. Most healthy people will score themselves between 70-80 on this scale, whereas cancer patients will typically score 30-40. The

'Cancer and its treatment can have very profound negative effects on your quality of life.'

assessment should be repeated at regular intervals throughout treatment which allows the doctor to determine how the quality of life changes. If it is getting worse then there are things that can be done to help. The importance of quality of life in cancer means that the Linear Analogue Scale and other similar assessment tools are being used outside of clinical trials and are becoming a routine part of clinical practice in hospitals around the UK.

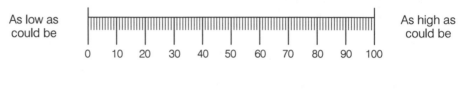

As low as
could be

As high as
could be

0   10   20   30   40   50   60   70   80   90   100

Same scale for:
- energy level
- ability to do daily activities

*Linear Analogue Scale Assessment (LASA) for
measurement of changes in quality of life*

A word about cancer-related fatigue

As I have mentioned earlier cancer and its treatment can have a negative effect on quality of life, such as your energy levels and your ability to do activities of normal daily living. I wanted to mention fatigue in particular as this seems to be an especially common and debilitating problem in people with cancer and it has a major impact on quality of life.

We tend to think of fatigue in broad terms as a sense of malaise (feeling generally unwell), tiredness, exhaustion or feeling sick. We have all experienced fatigue at some point in our lives so what's the big deal with cancer-related fatigue? Healthy people will typically feel exhausted and fatigued after sleep deprivation. But this is normal fatigue; if healthy people sleep, their fatigue disappears, and they feel recovered. People with diseases, even very common diseases (e.g. a simple flu), can feel extremely fatigued. Once the flu is over, however, the fatigue is gone. Fatigue in people with cancer is a very different concept. These people experience fatigue in relation to their therapy and their tumour that has very specific phenomena and that differs not only from fatigue in healthy people, but also from fatigue in people suffering from other diseases. A simple definition of cancer fatigue is that it is a feeling and a state of tiredness that exceeds the norm, is experienced as clearly unpleasant and does not improve with rest.

To give you an idea of how profoundly cancer-related fatigue can affect people a survey was conducted in three cancer treatment centres in Glasgow, Birmingham and Southampton. The findings were published in 2003. A total of 576 people with cancer attending outpatient clinics at the treatment centres completed a questionnaire and the results of this survey are dramatic. Fatigue was reported in more than half the people who took part in the survey (58%) and it affected them significantly more than any other symptom they reported (such as pain and nausea/vomiting). More than half (52%) never discussed fatigue with their doctor and almost half (47%) felt that fatigue was just something they had to put up with. As a result only 14% of people said that they had been offered any treatment for their fatigue. One third of people reported that, unlike pain and nausea/vomiting, the symptoms of their fatigue were poorly controlled.

Perhaps the best way of understanding how cancer-related fatigue affects people is to see how they describe it. Here are some comments from people with cancer who suffered from fatigue:

'Fatigue doesn't just mean being tired. Fatigue is truly the full depression of the body's functions.'

'I have a lot of frustrations and anger over not feeling like doing ordinary things.'

'I was too tired to think . . . '

Cancer-related fatigue is still poorly understood and there appear to be a number of causes. The disease itself and its treatment can cause fatigue, as can pain and anaemia (these last two can be treated medically and the fatigue is often improved, which in turn improves quality of life). One of the more worrying aspects of cancer-related fatigue is that it can affect a person's willingness to continue with treatment for their cancer, especially if their fatigue has worsened significantly since starting treatment or has been caused by the treatment.

Fatigue can be managed and there are a number of interventions that can help. If you are anaemic and your haemoglobin level is low, correcting the anaemia has been shown to be advantageous and improves fatigue and quality of life. If you are suffering from fatigue you should always plan your day so that you learn to conserve energy by building in time to rest and do the things that you most want to do – as doing things for yourself is very important. Exercise has been shown to help the symptoms of fatigue. Regular light exercise decreases fatigue and improves sleep. Although resting during the day is important, normal sleep patterns should be maintained, for example waking up at the same time each day. A poor diet can cause fatigue so maintaining your food intake is also important. Eating little and often throughout the day can help, drinking plenty of fluids, preparing extra meals when you have the energy. Keeping a diary is also useful as it can show whether your fatigue gets worse or better over time.

'Fatigue is the most common symptom reported by people with cancer and it has the biggest impact on quality of life.'

Most importantly, if you feel that you have fatigue and it doesn't get better with rest, talk to your doctor about it. As the results of the survey on the previous page show, many people do not mention fatigue to their doctor at all and if your doctor doesn't know that you have fatigue they cannot help you.

Summing Up

- Being given the news that you have cancer can be shocking and devastating, but it is important to put things into perspective.

- Cancer is becoming a treatable, long-term condition and more people are surviving it.

- If you are well informed about your cancer you will be better able to cope with it and any treatment.

- Be aware of the difference between remission and cure. A complete remission is almost as good as cure but is not quite the same thing.

- Surgery to remove part of your bowel might result in a stoma, but most of these are temporary and are very discreet.

- Nobody knows what having cancer is like unless they have had it themselves, but people are very supportive of those with cancer, so it is important to talk to others about your diagnosis.

- People who have had cancer themselves can offer tremendous emotional support, and counselling can be very valuable if you feel you cannot discuss your disease with the people closest to you.

- Having bowel cancer should not prevent you from continuing to work and there is plenty of guidance and support available on this subject.

- Bowel cancer and/or its treatment can have a negative effect on your quality of life and some treatment centres actively measure it so they can help you cope. It is important to talk to your doctor about negative changes in your quality of life.

- Fatigue is the most common symptom reported by people with cancer and it has the biggest impact on quality of life. It has a number of causes, some of which can be managed.

Chapter Seven

Bowel Cancer – A Survivor's Story

Introduction (author)

I wanted to write a book on bowel cancer although I have not had the disease myself, so I cannot really appreciate what it feels like to have bowel cancer and to live with it. I have a heart condition that has (so far) been successfully treated with surgery, so in a sense I have had a life-changing event because of a medical condition and there are some similarities with living with cancer: I have to cope with life every day with the knowledge that my condition might return at any time.

It is said we all know someone who has or has had cancer. I know of two people who have had bowel cancer and one of them, Mr B, very kindly offered to speak to me about his bowel cancer to add a patient perspective to this book. I am so very grateful for his help. This is his story.

Mr B's story

'I knew about bowel cancer as my mother had died from it, although she was 94 when she was diagnosed and it was so advanced there was little that the doctors could do for her at the time.

'I remember very clearly how I found out that I had got bowel cancer. In January 2007, I was decorating my eldest son's nursery in preparation for the arrival of our first grandchild, but I was unable to finish the job because I came down with what I thought was flu. I was tired, had hot sweats followed by shivers and could not eat. I lost a lot of weight in a very short time, which I put down to a change in diet as I had been diagnosed with Type 2 diabetes. After ten days or so, I didn't seem to be getting any better and then, one morning, I woke up and found a large soft lump about the size of a tennis ball! on the right side of my abdomen, just above my waistline. I was worried as it hadn't been there the night before. My wife rang the emergency doctor who advised us to go to the casualty department at the local hospital. I was admitted and had a series of X-rays and scans. The doctors were not sure what the problem was so in the end a surgeon carried out an exploratory operation to have a look inside my abdomen. The surgeon told me after the operation that my colon had split and some of the fluid had leaked out forming an abscess (the tennis ball-sized lump I'd found). He said that he had removed a piece of colon which contained a large tumour that had caused the split and he had also removed most of the abscess, although part of it had become stuck to the inner wall of my abdomen and couldn't be taken out. The surgeon had managed to sew the two ends of colon straight back together, meaning I did not have to have a stoma.

'The tumour and abscess were sent away to be analysed and the results for the tumour came back the day before I was due to go home. The colorectal nurse came to see me and told me that the tumour was cancer, but the good news was that the tumour had already been removed. I was then referred to the cancer team and after an MRI scan I saw the cancer specialist who told me that he could not find any evidence of any cancer but, because of the fact that the colon had split and an abscess had formed that had not been completely removed, he could not be sure that there were no cancer cells remaining, so he offered me a choice of either a course of radiotherapy and chemotherapy, or I could walk away and not have any further treatment. I remembered that I had been decorating a nursery for my first grandchild when I had become unwell. I felt guilty and upset that I hadn't been able to finish the job but didn't want to consider the possibility that I might not be around to see my grandchild, so I accepted the treatment.

'I had 25 sessions of radiotherapy at one session a day starting in April 2007 and at the same time I started taking tablets of a chemotherapy drug called capecitabine. The radiotherapy made me feel very tired and I was unable to drive, so my wife and family had to take me to the hospital to have my treatment but I managed reasonably well with the capecitabine tablets to begin with (I'd been told that my hair might fall out but that didn't happen). But

'I remembered that I had been decorating a nursery for my first grandchild when I had become unwell. I felt guilty and upset that I hadn't been able to finish the job but didn't want to consider the possibility that I might not be around to see my grandchild, so I accepted the treatment.'

the one problem I did have was swelling and pain in my hands and feet from taking the tablets. This became so bad that at one point I was unable to stand up. I had to sleep with my feet outside the bedclothes because the pain was so bad and my feet were burning. I eventually had to stop taking the tablets a week and a half before I was due to finish the course because I couldn't tolerate the pain anymore.

'During the chemotherapy I was told that I had to avoid getting an infection at all costs as this would have delayed the chemotherapy treatment by a month. This was frustrating as I had always been active; I enjoyed walking, playing golf, cycling and gardening but now I could do none of those things, even if I hadn't been suffering from pain and swelling in my hands and feet. Unfortunately, the day after I finished my course of radiotherapy I developed a bowel infection. I had bouts of severe diarrhoea every half an hour or so during the day and night so I had to go back into hospital for antibiotics. Within a few days the infection had cleared up and, luckily, it didn't delay my next cycle of chemotherapy.

'For nine months of my life I was virtually housebound because of the chemotherapy and the risk of infection; it was hugely frustrating at times. I was told that I could exercise in moderation but I didn't feel up to it and spent most of my time at home doing jigsaws. When we did go out, I had to go out in the car and stay in the car. I felt depressed and angry but the one thing that I focussed on was being there for the birth of my grandchild. I also wanted to make sure that I was clear of the cancer.

'I had a series of follow-up visits to the cancer team at the hospital and every time I was told that there was no evidence of cancer, although nobody ever said I was cured. When my grandson was born it was hugely emotional and it made the pain, anger and frustration I'd experienced during radiotherapy and chemotherapy worthwhile. I have since had two more grandchildren and I would willingly go through it all again if it meant I could be around to watch them grow up. I am currently having follow-up appointments every year and next year I can stop seeing the specialists as it will have been five years since my diagnosis and I am still clear of the disease.

'Looking back on my experience I felt very lucky that my cancer had effectively been removed before it was diagnosed. Seeing other people with bowel cancer that were far more sick than I had been made me feel like a fraud at times and I came home thinking that I could, and should, put up with the

> **'Bowel cancer is not a killer and it can be treated, even cured. However the process of treating it can be hard and long . . . You must always have a focus in life . . . I believe that how you cope with cancer has a lot to do with your state of mind. You must never give up.'**

treatment I was having. I didn't know how long I'd lived with the cancer as, apart from the sudden weight loss, I had none of the symptoms normally associated with bowel cancer; I had no pain or blood loss and my bowel movements were normal. There is nothing as good as not knowing and if I had been diagnosed with cancer earlier, say by my GP, I probably wouldn't have been so accepting of the fact. In a way I didn't feel that I had cancer because at the time I was told that a tumour had been found in my colon it had already been taken away.

'I am 72 now and I am living life to the full. I used to love cycling and I haven't been on a bike since I had my operation to remove my tumour, but I want to do this again, even if I won't be able to ride as far as I could before. I go walking regularly and spend time in the garden but I always want to do more, as I am enjoying life so much now. Having had cancer has made me change my perspective on life.

'I have to manage my diet quite rigorously as my digestive system has got slower since my operation and sometimes food and gas can get trapped. I have to avoid certain foods such as tomatoes, mushrooms and anything very acidic and I now have to have smaller meals and my main meal at lunchtime, but this seems a small price to pay for getting my life back.

'The first thing I would say to somebody who has been diagnosed with bowel cancer is that it is not a killer and it can be treated, even cured. However, the process of treating it can be hard and long. You must always have a focus in life, such as your family or something that you want to achieve or carry on enjoying. I believe that how you cope with cancer has a lot to do with your state of mind. You must never give up. If you do you will sink into a dark abyss that you will never come out of.'

Chapter Eight

Further Information

Below is a list of further information and sources of further information on current and future developments in the diagnosis and treatment of bowel cancer.

DNA testing

A number of research groups around the world (including the USA and Europe) are working on DNA tests for colon cancer which would use either blood or stool samples to look for mutated genes that are linked to colon cancer. This approach could mean that a colonoscopy may become unnecessary, though at this stage the accuracy of the DNA tests is not known and there is little information on who should be offered them.

Clinical trials

For people whose bowel cancer cannot be cured or has not responded as well as expected to standard treatment, the opportunity to take part in a clinical trial on new treatments or combinations of treatments may be offered to you by your doctor. ClinicalTrials.gov is an American-based website that lists thousands of clinical research trials being conducted all around the world in a huge variety of diseases including cancer. Many of these studies are multinational and people from the UK will often be recruited into them. www.clinicaltrials.gov

Cancer Research UK has a clinical trial search page where you can look for clinical trials that are ongoing and recruiting patients. Information on the different types of trials, finding suitable trials and taking part in one is also provided here. www.cancerhelp.org.uk/trials/

The World Health Organisation EPIC project

The European Prospective Investigation into Cancer and Nutrition (EPIC) project has been designed to look at the relationships between diet, nutritional status, lifestyle and environmental factors on the incidence of cancer and other chronic diseases. So far the project has recruited more than 500,000 people in ten European countries including the UK. This is a long-term study, which began in 1992 and is expected to continue collecting information for at least another 10 years. The main findings of the EPIC project so far can be found on the EPIC website. epic.iarc.fr/index.php

Oncology Conferences and Symposia

Oncology is the study of cancer. There are a number of Oncology Conferences and Symposia that are held around the world and these are often the first places where the latest research data is shared amongst doctors and other health-care professionals who are involved in the management of bowel cancer.

The biggest of these conferences is the American Society of Clinical Oncology (ASCO), held in the USA in May every year, and tens of thousands of oncologists attend the congress from all over the world. The ASCO website is often the first place to find the most recent research news on cancer from studies being conducted globally and much of the information on the website is freely available to the public. www.asco.org/

Closer to home the European Association for Cancer Research (EACR) holds a congress every year in a European city. The website is a good source of new information on European cancer trials. www.eacr.org/about/index.php

Glossary

Adenocarcinoma
A cancer that starts in the gland (mucus-producing) cells in the bowel wall.

Adenoma
A tag of tissue growing in the bowel. See also polyp.

Adjuvant treatment
Any treatment given after the main or initial treatment. For example, if surgery is the primary treatment, chemotherapy given following surgery is adjuvant treatment.

Alopecia
Medical term for hair loss.

Anaemia
A decrease in the number of red blood cells in the body or a reduction in the amount of haemoglobin in the blood. Anaemia can result in tiredness and breathlessness.

Anastomosis
In surgery, a procedure that joins two structures, such as reconnecting two ends of the bowel after removal of a section of bowel that contains a tumour.

Anti-emetic
A drug given to help prevent nausea and vomiting.

Benign
Not cancerous.

Biopsy
A small sample of tissue taken for analysis.

Body Mass Index (BMI)
A measure of body mass as a function of body weight divided by the square of the height.

Bolus
The administration of a drug in a single large dose.

Carcinogen
A substance that can cause cancer.

Chronic
Long-lasting. Many diseases such as Crohn's disease and cancer are chronic conditions.

Colectomy
Surgery to remove part of the colon.

Colonoscopy
Examination of the entire colon using an endoscope.

Constipation
Infrequent bowel movements with stools that are hard and difficult to pass.

Crohn's disease
An inflammatory disease that can affect the entire GI tract.

CT scan
Computerised tomography scan which uses X-ray images that are displayed in 3D by computers.

Cure
In medical terms, the complete recovery from a disease or condition such that the disease or condition never comes back.

Debulking
In surgery, removing part of a tumour.

Dehydration
Excessive loss of fluid from the body.

Diabetes
A group of diseases in which the level of sugar in the blood is not properly controlled.

DNA
Deoxyribonucleic acid, the genetic material in all human cells.

Endocrine
Relating to hormones.

Endoscope
Special flexible tube containing a light and camera to examine the lining of the GI tract.

Enzyme
A protein that increases the rate of a chemical reaction.

Faeces
Another name for waste matter or poo.

Flexible sigmoidoscopy
Examination of the sigmoid colon and rectum using an endoscope.

Gene
A unit of heredity in a living organism, usually a sequence of DNA that produces a protein when it is copied (expressed).

Genetics
The study of genes and hereditary characteristics.

GI
Gastrointestinal.

GP
General practitioner, otherwise known as family doctor.

Gy
Gray – a unit of measurement of radiation dose.

Haem
A red pigment in blood cells that is involved in the transport of oxygen to the tissues. Haem gives meat its red colour and is part of the structure of haemoglobin.

Haemoglobin
A red-coloured protein containing iron that is found in red blood cells and carries oxygen to the body tissues.

Haemorrhoids
Swellings in the lining of the lower rectum and anus.

Incidence

A measure of the number of new cases of a certain condition, such as cancer, over a defined time period. Usually expressed as a rate (e.g. 50 cases per 1,000 people per year, or 5% per year). Not to be confused with prevalence, which is the total number of cases of a condition in the population at any one time.

Inflammation

Swelling and reddening, usually of body tissue in response to injury or trauma.

Infusion

Administration of drugs into a patient through a vein at a steady rate over a period of time.

Inoperable

Surgery cannot be performed without substantial risk to the patient.

Intravenous (IV)

Directly into a vein.

Laxative

A drug given to clear the bowels of any faeces.

Lymphatic system

A network of vessels in the body that carry tissue fluid (lymph). Part of the immune system.

Malaise

A feeling of being generally unwell.

Mesentery

A large membrane that surrounds the small and large bowel.

Metastasis

A tumour that contains cancer cells that have spread from their original site (e.g. bowel cancer cells in the liver).

MRI scan

Magnetic resonance imaging scans use a strong magnetic field to produce highly detail images of sections through the body.

Mutation

A fault or a mistake, usually in reference to cell division and reproduction.

Need2Know

Nausea
Feeling sick.

Neoadjuvant treatment
Treatment given before the main treatment. For example neoadjuvant chemotherapy may be given to shrink the tumour before removing it with surgery.

Obesity
The condition of being dangerously overweight.

Occult
Hidden.

Oncogene
A gene that has the potential to cause cancer, usually as a result of being mutated or over-expressed.

Oncologist
A doctor who specialises in the treatment of cancer.

Oncology
The study of cancer.

Oral
By mouth.

Palmar-plantar erythema
Redness, soreness and peeling of skin on the hands and feet, a side effect sometimes caused by chemotherapy drugs such as 5-FU.

Polyp
A tag of tissue growing in the bowel. See also adenoma.

Prevalence
A measure of the total number of cases of a condition such as cancer in the population at any one time. Not to be confused with incidence, which is the number of new cases of the condition.

Prodrug
A drug given in an inactive form that converts to its active form only when inside the body.

Regimen

A planned course of medical treatment.

Remission

Absence of any sign of a disease or condition. Remission can be complete (total absence of any detectable disease) or partial (for example 50% reduction in tumour size). Not to be confused with cure.

Screening

In medical terms, a process of trying to identify a disease or condition in people who have no symptoms.

Sedative

A drug given to help people relax, usually before a procedure such as colonoscopy or sigmoidoscopy.

Sensory peripheral neuropathy

A condition that affects sensory nerves causing tingling and/or numbness. A side effect of chemotherapy drugs such as oxaliplatin.

Squamous cell carcinoma

A tumour that starts in the cells of the lining of the bowel.

Staging

A method used by a doctor to determine the size of a tumour and whether it has spread.

Sternum

Breast bone, part of the ribcage in the human skeleton.

Stool

Waste matter (poo) that comes out of your bowels. See also Faeces.

Systemic

Throughout the body.

Tenesmus

A straining sensation in the rectum which can be painful and often results in an inability to pass stools.

Tumour

An abnormal growth of cells that may or may not be cancerous.

Tumour suppressor gene
A gene that can prevent a cell from becoming cancerous.

Ulcerative colitis
An inflammatory disease of the bowel that usually affects the large bowel.

Vein
Blood vessel that carries blood from the tissues back to the heart.

Vomiting
Being sick.

Help List

Beating Bowel Cancer

Harlequin House, 7 High Street, Teddington, TW11 8EE
Tel: 08450 719300 (Lo Call rate)
Fax: 020 8943 0629
www.beatingbowelcancer.org/
This is a UK charity dedicated to saving lives from bowel cancer. Beating Bowel Cancer raises awareness of the disease and provides support to patients and their families.

Bowel Cancer UK

7 Rickett Street
London
SW6 1RU
Tel: 0207381 9711
http//www.bowelcanceruk.org.uk

British Nutrition Foundation

High Holborn House, 52-54 High Holborn, London, WC1V 6RQ
Tel: 020 7404 6504
http://www.nutrition.org.uk/
The British Nutrition Foundation provides nutrition information for teachers, health professionals scientists, and the general public.

Cancer Research UK

Angel Building, 407 St John Street, London, EC1V 4AD
Tel: (Switchboard) 020 7242 0200
www.cancerresearchuk.org/
www.cancerhelp.org.uk/
For general information, the Cancer Research UK website is excellent. In addition to general information on the Cancer Research UK website, which can be accessed through Cancerhelp UK, the patient information section, you can also read about the latest clinical research trials in the treatment of bowel cancer. Simply click on the Cancerhelp UK Trials and Research tab and select Bowel Cancer from the trials drop-down list.

Department of Health

Richmond House, 79 Whitehall, London, SW1A 2NS
Tel: 020 7210 4850
www.dh.gov.uk/en/Healthcare/Cancer/index.htm
The Department of Health (DH) is the government organisation for public health issues. The DH provides information which is mainly for use by health-care professionals but much of the information is available to the public, including a cancer portal, which contains useful links and information about the government strategy for cancer in the UK, screening, treatment and waiting times, among other subjects.

Directgov

www.direct.gov.uk/en/index.htm
This is a government website that provides useful information on benefits and financial support for those with long-term conditions such as cancer. Contact details for services local to you can be found through the website.

Food and Drink Federation

6 Catherine Street, London, WC2B 5JJ
Tel: 020 7836 2460
www.fdf.org.uk/
The Food and Drink Federation (FDF) represents the interests of the UK's food and non-alcoholic drinks manufacturing industry and specific food sectors.

Macmillan Cancer Support

89 Albert Embankment, London, SE1 7UQ
Tel: 0808 808 00 00
www.macmillan.org.uk/Home.aspx
Macmillan Cancer Support is a voluntary organisation that provides practical, medical and financial support for people living with cancer. Macmillan has a national presence so you should be able to find help and support close to you. The website has a huge amount of useful information on all aspects of cancer.

National Institute for Clinical Excellence (NICE)

MidCity Place, 71 High Holborn, London, WC1V 6NA
Tel: 0845 003 7780
The NICE guidance on the screening of bowel cancer can be found at:
http://egap.evidence.nhs.uk/cg118
NICE is a government organisation that produces guidance on the treatment of many diseases based on the best evidence available.

NHS Bowel Cancer Screening Programme (BCSP)

Fulwood House, Old Fulwood Road, SHEFFIELD, S10 3TH
Tel: 0114 271 1060
www.bcsp.nhs.uk
The NHS BCSP website contains detailed and helpful information on the bowel cancer screening programme throughout the UK.

NHS Change4Life

Tel: 0300 123 4567
www.nhs.uk/change4life/Pages/change-for-life.aspx
The NHS Change4Life website was designed to encourage adults and children to get fit and active, eating well, moving more and living longer as a result. The website contains lots of tips and useful information on healthy eating and exercise. It is a good way of finding activities in your local area that you might wish to join.

NHS Choices

www.nhs.uk/conditions/Cancer-of-the-colon-rectum-or-bowel/Pages/Introduction.aspx

You can find information on bowel cancer using the NHS Choices website by clicking the Health A-Z tab, then clicking B, followed by the Bowel Cancer link. There is a short video by Celia Ingham Clarke, a consultant surgeon at the Whittington hospital in London, who explains bowel cancer and its treatment in a clear, friendly and understandable way. Alternatively, the link above will take you straight to the bowel cancer page.

Patient Voices (Beating Bowel Cancer)

Tel: 020 8973 0014

www.beatingbowelcancer.org/patient-voices

Patient Voices is the only UK national patient-to-patient network offering help to people and their relatives affected by bowel cancer. Patient Voices provides one-to-one support by people who have had a diagnosis of bowel cancer and wish to help others. Further information can be found on the Beating Bowel Cancer website.

Book List

Cancer and its Management.
Souhami, Robert and Tobias, Jeffrey. Blackwell Publishing, 2003 Fourth Edition.
ISBN: 0 632 05531 6

Cancer as Initiation: Surviving the Fire.
Stone, Barbara. Open Court Publishing, 1995. Second Edition.
ISBN: 0 8126 9274 8

Cancer is a Word, not a Sentence: A positive and supportive guide for patients, families and friends.
Castle, Fiona. Hodder & Stoughton, 2000. ISBN: 0 340 74565 7

Cancer Treatment and Care: A Guide for Patients, Families and Carers.
Lynn, Joan. Northcote House, 1992. ISBN: 0 7463 0581 8

Comprehensive Cancer Care: Integrating Alternative, Complementary and Conventional Therapies.
Gordon, James S and Curtin, Sharon. Perseus Publishing, 2001.
ISBN: 0 7382 0486 2

Clinical Oncology – Basic Principles and Practice.
Neal, Anthony J, Hoskin, Peter J. Oxford University Press, 2003. Third Edition. ISBN: 0 340 76409 0

Cancer: What every patient needs to know.
Tobias, Jeffrey. Bloomsbury Publishing, 1995. ISBN: 0 7474 4565 0

Fatigue in Cancer: European School of Oncology Scientific Updates, 5
Marty, M and Pecorelli, S. Elsevier Publishing, 2001. ISBN: 0 444 50905 4

Living with Cancer: symptoms, diagnosis, treatment.
Tobias, Jeffrey and Eaton, Kay. Bloomsbury Publishing, 2001.
ISBN: 0 7475 5410 2

Supportive Cancer Care: The Complete Guide for Patients and Their Families.
Rosenbaum, Ernest H and Rosenbaum, Isadora. Sourcebooks Inc. 2001. ISBN: 1 57071 787 7

What you really need to know about cancer: A guide for patients and their families
Buckman, Robert. Key Porter Books. 1995. ISBN: 0 330 33628 2

Weight Loss – The Essential Guide
Kirkham, Sarah. Need2Know 2010. ISBN: 978-1-86144-090-7

References

Atkin WS, Edwards R, Kralj-Hans I et al. Once-only flexible sigmoidoscopy screening in prevention of colorectal cancer: a multicentre randomised controlled trial. Lancet 2010;375(9726):1624-1633.

Park Y, Subar AF, Hollenbeck A, Schatzkin A. Dietary Fiber Intake and Mortality in the NIH-AARP Diet and Health Study. Arch Intern Med 2011.

Rothwell PM, Wilson M, Elwin CE et al. Long-term effect of aspirin on colorectal cancer incidence and mortality: 20-year follow-up of five randomised trials. Lancet 2010;376(9754):1741-1750.

Schutze M, Boeing H, Pischon T et al. Alcohol attributable burden of incidence of cancer in eight European countries based on results from prospective cohort study. BMJ 2011;342:d1584.

Stone P, Ream E, Richardson A et al. Cancer-related fatigue--a difference of opinion? Results of a multicentre survey of healthcare professionals, patients and caregivers. Eur J Cancer Care (Engl) 2003;12(1):20-27.

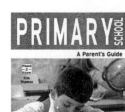

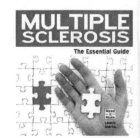